OCTOBER

Make the Most of Every Month with Carson-Dellosa's Monthly Books!

Production Manager
Chris McIntyre

Editorial Director
Jennifer Weaver-Spencer

Writers
Lynette Pyne
Amy Gamble
Lynn Ruppard
Karen M. Smith

Editors
Maria McKinney
Kelly Gunzenhauser
Carol Layton

Art Director
Penny Casto

Art Coordinator
Edward Fields

Carson-Dellosa Art Adaptations
Erik Huffine
David Lackey
Ray Lambert
Betsy Peninger
Pam Thayer
Todd Tyson
Julie Webb

Cover Design
Amber Kocher Crouch
Ray Lambert
J.J. Rudisill

D1247438

Carson-Dellosa Publishing Company, Inc.

OCTOBER

Table of Contents

OCTOBER TEACHER TIPS

Classroom Helpers
Make an easy-to-use job assignment chart using poster board and clothespins. Write out a two-column list of students' names on poster board with one column on the far left side and the other column on the far right side. Write the names of classroom jobs on clothespins. Clip the clothespin to the edge of the poster board beside the name of the child assigned to that classroom job. Change the job assignments by moving the clothespins to different names.

Checking Out Centers
Use this idea to check student attendance at classroom learning centers. Decide which students in your class would benefit from which learning centers. Place a large plastic cup at each classroom center. Clip four or five clothespins labeled with student names around the top of the cup. When a student has visited a center, have him remove his clip and drop it inside the cup.

Organize Worksheets
Organize seasonal worksheets using cardboard magazine boxes. Label each magazine box with a holiday or theme. Clip together worksheets that cover skills related to the theme. Refer to the files when writing lesson plans for a quick reference of available worksheets.

Display Tree
Make a festive classroom display tree using a large cardboard carpet roll. Cut tree branches from heavy paper and attach them to the top of the roll using a hot glue gun. Cut out and glue fall colored leaves to the branches. Tape student work around the tree trunk to create a 3-D work display.

Game Storage
Game storage is simple with this idea. Store desktop games and learning centers in large plastic dishpans. Use clear packing tape to attach a label containing the name of the game or center. When the games are not in use, stack the containers for easy storage.

Seasonal Word Walls
Create a word wall to use during the month. Cut out simple seasonal shapes from colored paper and label each one with a seasonal word. Post the shapes and let students use the words in their writing throughout the month.

October

Day-by-Day Calendar

1 *World Vegetarian Day* Have your students plan a balanced vegetarian meal. Celebrate with a meatless lunch which might include macaroni and cheese or bean burritos.

2 The comedian *Julius "Groucho" Marx* was born on this day in 1895. Invite each student to tell a joke in his honor.

3 *National Caramel Month* Bring in caramel squares, caramel-coated apples, candy bars, etc., and have a party in honor of this sweet treat.

4 *Sputnik I* was the first successful artificial Earth satellite launched, marking the beginning of the Space Age in 1957. Have students write journals as if they were on Sputnik I.

5 *National Storytelling Festival Day* Have students write stories for a classroom book. Discuss what makes a good storyteller (gestures, props, etc.). After the stories are complete, have students present their stories.

6 *German-American Day* Teach students common German phrases such as *Guten Morgan* (Good Morning) or *Danke* (Thank You). Play a German tape and encourage students to try a few German words during free time.

7 *Rose is National Flower* In 1985, President Ronald Reagan signed a bill making the rose the United States' national flower. Ask students if they think the rose was a good choice. Why or why not?

8 *National Chili Week* takes place the first full week in October. Bring in a crock pot and have students provide the ingredients to make chili.

9 *Adopt-A-Shelter-Animal Month* Invite students to make posters encouraging people to adopt an animal from a shelter.

10 *National Dental Hygiene Month* Ask a dentist to come in and talk to the class about dental hygiene.

11 *Kathryn Sullivan* became the *first woman to walk in space* aboard the sixth Challenger flight in 1984. Have students write or tell something they would like to do before anyone else.

12 *Global Scream Day* Take the class outside and have the students see if they can scream for 15 seconds.

13 *National Train Your Brain Day* Pass out brainteasers for students to figure out. Have older students write their own.

14 *e.e. cummings'* (he wrote his name in lowercase letters) *birthday.* In his poetry, cummings makes up words by combining existing words. (everyanything, for example.) Read a poem to the class and ask students to make up their own words.

15 *Computer Learning Month* Have students complete a story titled *What My Computer Taught Me!*

4

16 *World Rainforest Week* Introduce students to rainforest animals and plants such as jaguars, toucans, orchids, etc. Ask students to draw a rainforest scene including their favorites.

17 *Hunger Awareness Month* If possible, have students bring in food to donate to a local shelter.

18 *Alaska Day* The transfer of Alaska from Russia to the U.S. was official on this day in 1867. Have students practice research skills to find out facts about Alaska, such as the state flower, exports, etc. Organize the information the students find out into a web or an outline.

19 *Month of the Dinosaur* Encourage students to bring in pictures, stuffed animals, books, and other items that celebrate dinosaurs and have them share with the class.

20 P.T. Barnum opened the Hippodrome in New York, home of the *"Greatest Show On Earth."* Have children draw or tell their favorite circus memory. If they have never been, have them draw what they think it might be like and tell why they would or would not like to go.

21 *National Stamp Collecting Month* Invite students to bring in stamp collections to share with the class.

22 The first *Society of Whale Watchers* was established in 1951 to save these animals from extinction. Have students design posters promoting the Society of Whale Watchers.

23 *Book Fair Month* Organize a book fair with the class to be held at your school library.

24 Commemorate the last ride of the *Pony Express* in 1861 by delivering a letter to another teacher pony-express style. Line students up between the classroom and the letter's destination. Hand off the letter until it is delivered.

25 *Make a Difference Day* Make a class list of ways to make a difference. Then, as a class, complete one of them.

26 *Steven Kellogg's Birthday* Share one of his tall tales, such as *Paul Bunyan*, with your class.

27 James Cook, the English sea captain who discovered the Hawaiian Islands, was born in 1728. Have students make leis with tissues paper flowers in his honor.

28 The *Statue of Liberty* was dedicated in 1886. Teach the class about the famous statue and the freedom for which it stands.

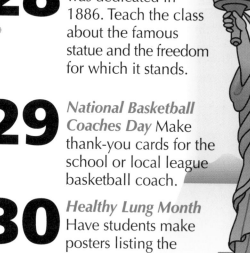

29 *National Basketball Coaches Day* Make thank-you cards for the school or local league basketball coach.

30 *Healthy Lung Month* Have students make posters listing the dangers of smoking. Hang the posters around the classroom or school.

31 *Mt. Rushmore* was completed on October 31. Have students draw a *Mt. (Last Name)* with family members "carved" into a mountain.

October

Sunday	Monday	Tuesday	Wednesday	Thursday	Friday	Saturday

Read In October!

Dear Family Members,
Here are some books to share with your child to enhance the enjoyment of reading in October.

 Red Leaf, Yellow Leaf by Lois Ehlert
- *A child shares a scrapbook describing the life cycle of a maple tree from a seed to an ever growing tree, then shares a favorite leaf from the tree.*
- Go on a walk to collect leaves with your child, then use them to make an autumn leaf booklet.

 When the Frost is on the Punkin by James Whitcomb Riley
- *A child enjoys an autumn morning on a farm. The text is a classic read-aloud poem celebrating autumn changes.*
- Have your child clap out the rhythm of the story as you read it aloud.

 Pumpkin Fiesta by Caryn Yacowitz
- *Foolish Fernando decides he can grow better pumpkins than Old Juana and thinks he has figured out her secret.*
- Have your child predict what will happen each time Foolish Fernando tries to outwit Old Juana.

 The Ghost-Eye Tree by Bill Martin, Jr. and John Archambault
- *Two children take a journey past the dreaded ghost-eye tree, where their imaginations run wild.*
- Challenge your child to find the cat hidden on each page of the story.

 The Little Scarecrow Boy by Margaret Wise Brown
- *A scarecrow boy wants to help his father in the cornfield, but his father tells him he is not fierce-looking enough to scare a crow.*
- Ask your child to name something he wishes he could do but is too young. Then, have him name some things he can do well already.

 Possum's Harvest Moon by Anne Hunter
- *When Possum wakes up one autumn night and sees the bright harvest moon, he decides to have a moonlit party for his forest friends.*
- Have a harvest party with your child, complete with apple juice and cookies.

 Dem Bones by Bob Barner
- *This classic African-American story also includes factual information about bones.*
- Take turns with your child naming different bones and pointing out where they are located.

Pick of the Patch
Nice Work!

Name _____

Signed _____

Date _____

_____

HAS A
NEAT DESK!

READING

MATH

My Pencils

SCIENCE

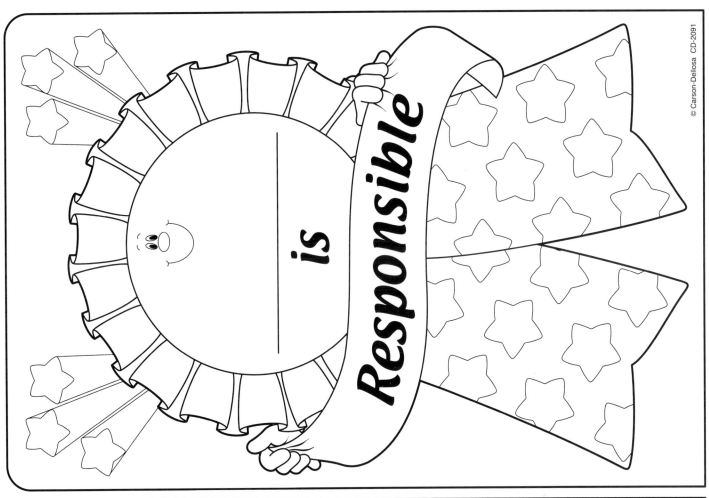

is

Responsible

We missed you!
Here's what you missed!

_____
_____
_____
_____
_____
_____

OCTOBER
Writing Activities

October is a great time to inspire beginning writers! Encourage students to notice subtle changes this month — the softer slant of light, grasses and wildflowers going to seed, and hot soup tasting better than it did in July. While students are writing about October, enjoy its beauty with them firsthand. Go outside for awhile—and just smile!

Word Bank Words

leaves	bat	scarecrow
color	owl	spider
tree	harvest	costume
pumpkin	squirrel	skeleton
autumn	acorn	

Spelling Word Search

Let students puzzle over spelling words! Give students copies of a simple grid with squares that are large enough for writing letters. Have them make word searches using spelling words, then exchange them with classmates to solve. Have students write out the words as they find them.

```
O C H I L L Y N M
L T K J E I H G F
B C R D A E B I H
A Z Y E V X W A T
S C A R E C R C V
U T O S S R O W
S K E L E Q R P
N M L E T O N O
G F E K O J W I H
  E D C R L B A
```

Use Your Senses

Students can learn how to be "sense"ative with this activity. Have students write about an autumn day and challenge them to describe it using their five senses. Have them write about the colors, smells, tastes, sounds, and feelings of an autumn day. Have them use metaphors (figures of speech in which analogies are made between two objects) such as *drowning in money*, in their writings.

Fall Fun

Fall is a time for fun! Have students write about something fun they like to do in the fall. Have them write their final drafts on large colorful leaf shapes cut from construction paper.

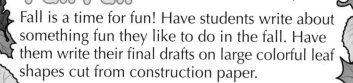

In the fall I like to rake leaves. Then I like to jump in them.

I like to look at the tree colors in fall. I like to put on a mask and scare people, too.

UNWANTED WORDS

Write all about it! Challenge students by having them write about a topic without using specific words. For example, have them write a short story about a hayride without using the words *hay*, *wagon*, or *ride*.

BIG REWARD
IF WORD IS NOT USED

Dear Fall Tree

Dear Tree.... Have each student write a letter to a fall tree persuading the tree not to shed its leaves. Encourage them to list reasons why the tree should keep its leaves all the time.

Orange leaves fall to the ground.
Cider is made from apples.
Trick-or-treat!
Owls hoot in the trees at night.
Birds fly south for the winter
Everyone wears sweaters.
Ride in a wagon full of hay.

October Acrostic Booklets

Fall poetry will add color to any classroom. Tell students to write October down the left-hand side of a piece of paper. Have younger students write a fall-related word beginning with each letter. Older students can write a descriptive sentence beginning with each letter. For instance, *Orange leaves fall softly to the ground – Cider made from apples cools my thirst,* etc. Allow students to make booklets to showcase their October acrostics.

Eek, a Mystery!

Encourage students to be mysterious! Have students write short mystery stories about a dark October night. For added fun, turn out the classroom lights and let each student read his story to the class by flashlight.

A Book of Difficult Words to Spell

Teach spelling with a twist. Have students keep a list of all the difficult, misspelled words that proofreaders mark. Give each student a booklet and have them write the correct spelling for each word. Encourage students to refer to their "Mis"spelling Books when writing.

Bulletin Board Ideas

Students will go nuts over this adorable display! Cover the top ²/₃ of a bulletin board with sky blue paper and the bottom ¹/₃ with green paper. Enlarge the squirrel pattern (page 30) on gray paper and place it on the bulletin board. Enlarge several acorn patterns (page 30) on brown paper and write fall-related words on them such as *squirrel, autumn, scarecrow, acorn, tree, leaf, pumpkin,* etc. Place the completed acorns on the bulletin board as a word bank for autumn writing exercises. This bulletin board may be used with the *Falling Into Autumn* chapter (pages 20-32).

Give your students something to crow about with this scarecrow display. Cover the bulletin board with light green paper. Enlarge, cut out, and construct the scarecrow pattern (page 32). Provide old fabric scraps and bits of yarn and a straw hat and let students work on decorating the scarecrow. Display the scarecrow on the bulletin board. Cut tall, dome-shaped haystacks from yellow construction paper and glue on bits of hay, raffia, or yellow yarn. Display outstanding student work on the haystacks. Title the bulletin board *Our Work Really Stacks Up!* This display may be used to accent the *Falling Into Autumn* chapter (pages 20-32).

14

Spark student imaginations with this fire safety bulletin board. Cover the bulletin board with yellow paper. Enlarge a magnifying glass pattern (page 47) and place it in the center. Have each student draw and color a fire hazard condition such as keeping pot holders away from burners, not placing electrical cords under rugs, etc., on a construction paper circle. Post the pictures around the magnifying glass. This display goes well with the *Get Fired Up About Fire Safety* chapter (pages 38-47).

Students will stop, drop, and roll for this display. Cover $1/3$ of the bulletin board with red paper, $1/3$ with orange paper, and $1/3$ with yellow paper. Have students help you create pretend three-dimensional red, yellow, and orange flames across the bottom with crumpled and rolled tissue paper, colored foil, and construction paper. Divide students into three groups. Take pictures of the students in the first group illustrating *stopping*. Take pictures of the students in the second group *dropping* to the ground. Finally, take photos of the children in the third group *rolling*. Divide the bulletin board into three sections, titled *Stop, Drop, and Roll* and place the appropriate photographs in the correct sections. Use this bulletin board to accent the *Get Fired Up About Fire Safety* chapter (pages 38-47).

Chart a course to success with this Columbus Day display. Cover the top ¼ of the bulletin board with light blue paper and the bottom ¼ with dark blue paper. Using an overhead projector, enlarge the ship pattern (page 53) onto white bulletin board paper. Have students color the enlarged pattern. Post it on the bulletin board along with excellent student work. You may want to display this bulletin board during the *In 1492:Columbus Day* unit (pages 48-55).

Just like Columbus, students can travel to new lands with this bulletin board! Cover the top half of a bulletin board with sky blue paper and the bottom half with royal blue paper. Create an island with tan paper. You can add palm trees made from green and brown paper. Have students or small groups of students choose travel-related books about places they have never been. After reading the book, have each student or group of students design a travel poster highlighting interesting facts, landmarks, and sites to visit. Display the completed posters accented with an enlarged ship pattern (page 53) around the island. Title the bulletin board *Travel to New Lands*. This display accents the *In 1492:Columbus Day* chapter (pages 48-55) well.

Dish out praise with this tasty bulletin board display. Cover the bottom half of a bulletin board with gingham cloth or a checked tablecloth. Cover the top half with sky blue paper. Give each child a small paper plate and provide materials such as markers, yarn, and construction paper scraps. Have children decorate their plates to resemble their favorite foods. Accent outstanding student papers with each paper plate. To add a chef's hat, cut a white strip from construction paper. Staple the strip to the bulletin board. Gather the edges of several pieces of white tissue paper above the construction paper strip to resemble the chef's hat. Display this bulletin board with the *Octoberfeast* chapter (pages 62-71).

Use this display to create pumpkin patch kids! Cover the top half of a bulletin board with sky blue paper and the bottom half with green paper. Enlarge two pumpkin patterns (page 84) for each student. On one pattern, have each child draw a picture of herself and write her name at the bottom. On the other, have her draw a picture of herself in a costume. Attach each child's costume picture on top of her other picture. Have students look at a costumed picture, guess which classmate is represented, and lift up the top pumpkin pattern to find out! You can add green construction paper leaves and twisted green bulletin board paper to resemble a pumpkin vine. Title the display, *Look Who's in the Pumpkin Patch!* This display complements the *Pumpkin Patch Fun* chapter (pages 75-86).

17

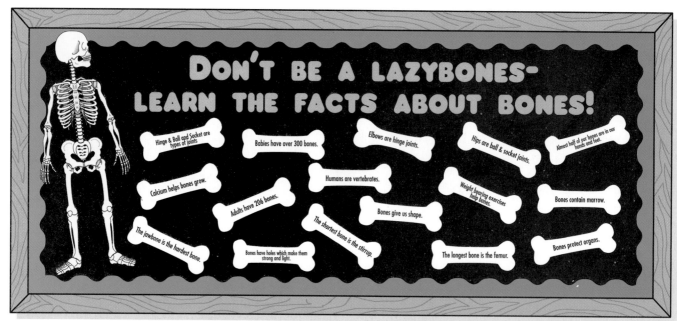

DON'T BE A LAZYBONES- LEARN THE FACTS ABOUT BONES!

Hinge & Ball and Socket are types of joints.

Babies have over 300 bones.

Elbows are hinge joints.

Hips are ball & socket joints.

Almost half of our bones are in our hands and feet.

Calcium helps bones grow.

Humans are vertebrates.

Weight bearing exercises help bones.

Bones contain marrow.

Adults have 206 bones.

Bones give us shape.

The jawbone is the hardest bone.

The shortest bone is the stirrup.

Bones have holes which make them strong and light.

The longest bone is the femur.

Bones protect organs.

No bones about it, students will bone up on skeleton and human body facts with this bulletin board. Cover the bulletin board with black paper. Display a large plastic skeleton or use the skeleton from the *Co"operation" Skeleton Display* (page 79). Give each student a copy of the bone pattern (page 85) and have him write a fact about bones or taking care of his bones on the pattern. Display the bones around the skeleton. You may wish to display this bulletin board with the *Bones* section of the *Pumpkin Patch Fun* unit (pages 75-86).

Get caught in this creative spiderweb bulletin board. Cover the bulletin board with dark blue or black paper. Hang white yarn or string across the bulletin board and pin the string on the bulletin board with straight pins to resemble a spiderweb. Allow each student to create a unique spider with construction paper, pipe cleaners, wiggly eyes, paint, etc., and print her name on the completed spider. Then, have students hang their spiders on the web. This bulletin board works well with the *Spiders* section of the Pumpkin Patch Fun chapter (pages 75-86).

WELCOME TO OUR WEB!

Betsy

Ray

Alex

Rosa

John

Kenny

Travis

Rhonda

David

Students will know whooo's out at night with this crafty display. Create this eye-catching bulletin board to display information and pictures of nocturnal animals along with completed activities and crafts from the *Nocturnal Neighbors* chapter (pages 87-92). Provide white bulletin board paper the same size as your bulletin board and allow students to paint or draw a nighttime forest scene with trees, stars, and the moon. Students can add glitter to make the moon and stars sparkle. After the nighttime scene has dried, place it on your bulletin board.

Students can learn important facts with this interactive display. Cover the bulletin board with black paper. Make a large tree on the left side of the bulletin board from brown bulletin board paper, and extend two limbs across the bulletin board. Enlarge 10-12 owl patterns (page 92) and staple half on the top limb and half on the bottom limb. Write questions such as *What is our state capital?, What is the name of a nocturnal bird?*, etc., on construction paper cut into the shape of speech balloons. Place one speech balloon beside each owl. Then, fold one small piece of paper in half for each question and write the answers to the questions on the inside of the folded paper. Next, attach the correct answer to each owl. Students can approach the bulletin board display, answer the questions, and raise the flaps to check their answers. This display works well with the *Nocturnal Neighbors* chapter (pages 87-92).

Falling Into Autumn

Leaves and Trees

Autumn is a great time of year to observe nature. In most parts of the country, leaves turn vibrant colors and fall to the ground, squirrels gather acorns for the winter ahead, and scarecrows protect fall crops. Autumn is not only perfect for learning about leaves, trees, squirrels, and scarecrows, but also for falling into fun!

Did You Know?

- Trees make their own food. Leaves use light from the sun, water from the ground, and carbon dioxide from the air to make a kind of sugar. This food-making process is called photosynthesis.

- Leaves are green because of a substance called chlorophyll, which also makes the tree's food.

- The more sugar in a leaf, the more red the leaf will turn in the autumn.

- Bright autumn colors exist in leaves all year long, but are hidden by chlorophyll during spring and summer.

Literature Selections

The Oak Tree by Paula Z. Hogan: Raintree Stech-Vaughn Publishers, 1986. (Picture book, 32 pg.) Easy-to-read description of an oak tree's life cycle.

Autumn Across America by Seymour Simon: Hyperion Press, 1993. (Picture book, 32 pg.) Describes fall across the United States.

Look What I Did with a Leaf by Morteza E. Sohi: Walker and Co., 1995. (Picture book, 32 pg.) Ideas for making pictures with leaves, plus information about leaves.

"Tree"-riffic Display

Climb into a study of trees and leaves by creating a realistic classroom tree! Sketch a life-size trunk and branches on paper grocery bags or brown bulletin board paper, then construct the tree on a wall. Add copies of the leaf patterns (page 32) on green or fall-colored construction paper to create a display to last through the year. As students complete activities, showcase their "tree"-mendous work "falling" from your new display.

EVERGREEN VS. DECIDUOUS

What's the difference between evergreen and deciduous trees? All trees replace their leaves over time as they become worn out. Leaves of deciduous trees, like maples, change colors and "fall" each autumn. Evergreens, like pines, replace their leaves gradually throughout the year so the process is not noticeable. Gather pictures of trees from magazines and have students guess if the trees are evergreen or deciduous. Write facts and characteristics of trees on tree patterns (page 30). Then, post the pictures on a bulletin board and let students match the facts to the correct type of tree.

Evergreen Tree Facts

- Most leaves are needlelike
- Branches are flexible
- Leaves stay green all year
- Used to decorate at Christmas
- Leaves are thick and waxy

Deciduous Tree Facts

- Leaves turn colors in autumn
- Branches don't bend easily
- Dormant in winter
- Lose all leaves at one time of year
- Leaves are thin and flat

Do Leaves Have Skeletons?

Answer this question by revealing a leaf's backbone! Leaves have skeletons which are the veins that carry water and food between the leaves and the branches. Let students look at leaves and find the veins. You can also see the veins by holding leaves up to light. Let students make leaf skeletons from fall-colored construction paper. Fold the paper in half lengthwise and draw half of a leaf (including a stem) and an outline of the veins, starting and ending at the fold. Then, carefully cut out the leaf and veins. When students unfold their papers, they will have two pieces, the leaf with the veins missing and the vein skeleton. Glue these side by side on a contrasting piece of paper. To make a real leaf skeleton, boil a leaf for 1$\frac{1}{2}$ hours, let it stand in water for several days, then remove the fleshy part with a small paintbrush.

Why Do Leaves Change Color?

As days become shorter and leaves get less sunlight, green chlorophyll drains away and leaves begin changing color. Make autumn arrive early by covering a green leaf. Take the class outside and find a leaf on a tree that students can reach. (If this is not possible, try the experiment with an indoor plant.) Record the location and color of the leaf. Paper clip a dark construction paper circle on top of the leaf. After several days, remove the paper and observe the yellowish pigments under the green chlorophyll. Ask students to record their observations and explain what happened.

21

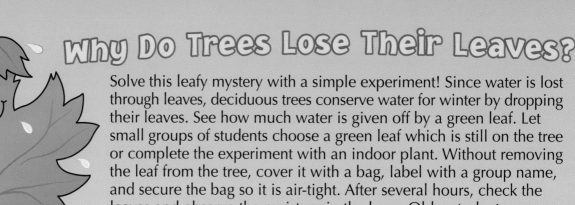

Why Do Trees Lose Their Leaves?

Solve this leafy mystery with a simple experiment! Since water is lost through leaves, deciduous trees conserve water for winter by dropping their leaves. See how much water is given off by a green leaf. Let small groups of students choose a green leaf which is still on the tree or complete the experiment with an indoor plant. Without removing the leaf from the tree, cover it with a bag, label with a group name, and secure the bag so it is air-tight. After several hours, check the leaves and observe the moisture in the bags. Older students can measure the water and estimate how much water their leaf would produce in a week, month, or year.

Lifetime of a Leaf

Just like humans, leaves grow up! A leaf begins its life inside a bud. In spring, small, light green leaves and sometimes flowers emerge from the buds. By summer, leaves are full-grown and dark green. In autumn, leaves turn colors and fall from the tree. Glue the four rectangles side by side on the cardboard. Glue a twig diagonally across each rectangle. As in panel 1, which represents a tree in winter, make brown tissue paper balls and glue them to the first twig for buds. On panel 2, glue tiny tissue paper leaves and flowers to show spring. Cut large summer leaves from tissue paper and glue them to the twig on panel 3. On panel 4, glue colorful leaves cut from red, orange, brown, and yellow tissue paper to represent autumn. Let the glue dry completely and display the projects on a bulletin board titled *A Leaf's Life*.

Materials

Before beginning, provide each student with a 21" x 8" piece of cardboard, four 4" x 6" light blue construction paper rectangles with torn edges, colored tissue paper, four 6" twigs, glue, and scissors.

Autumn Observations

Autumn is the perfect time to observe nature with a class nature walk. Bring paper, crayons, pencils, collecting bags, a tape recorder, and a camera. Stress that students should be quiet observers and only collect seeds, twigs, leaves, etc., from the ground. If necessary, explain what students should not collect, such as insects, garbage, etc. Encourage students to take notes about what they see, hear, smell, and touch during the walk. Record autumn sounds and let each student take a picture. Let students share the materials they collected in order of the five senses. Put the materials on a table to create a class display. Have students write descriptive words and phrases from their notebooks on leaf patterns (page 32) and include the patterns, recorded sounds, and photographs in the *Autumn Observations* display.

Nature Sounds

How Do Trees Travel?

Pack your imagination and learn how seeds travel! Ask students to come to the *Autumn Observations* (page 22) display and point to the seeds they collected. Discuss the different ways seeds travel (see below for details). Let each student choose his favorite seed and write an imaginative story about the seed's journey from the tree to the classroom.

Ways Seeds Travel!

- Light and airy seeds are blown in the wind.
- Spiky or sticky seeds attach to animals' fur.
- Seeds of fruit-bearing trees, such as apples and peaches, are spread by the animals that eat the fruit.
- Maple seeds are shaped like helicopter blades and spin and fly through the air.
- Acorns fall straight down from the tree and are carried away by squirrels and other animals.

First Team There Gets the Leaves

Team members cooperate to bag leaves in this relay race! Place two equal piles of fall leaves, artificial fall leaves, or copies of the leaf patterns (page 32), approximately 15 feet from the teams. Give the first child on each team a pair of tongs. Signal start and have the first student on each team run to the pile of leaves, pick up as many as he can with the tongs, and run back to the line. The leaves should be deposited in a brown grocery bag and the tongs given to the second student in line, who should run to the pile, pick up leaves with the tongs, run back, and so on. The winning team has all of its leaves in the bag first.

Ode to a Leaf

Rake up a pile of leaf-shaped poetry to celebrate autumn! Brainstorm with the class words, phrases, and sentences about leaves. On construction paper, let students sketch or trace a large leaf and draw in veins. Have students write poems containing the phrases and sentences around the outside edges of the leaf and along the vein lines. Write over the words in black pen so that the words form the leaf shape, then erase the original lines. Allow students to decorate their leaves and share their poems. After each student shares her poem, allow her to display it on a branch of your *"Tree"-riffic Display* (page 20).

That's My Tree!

Let students "adopt" trees to observe. Take students outside, break them into small groups, and let each group choose a tree. Distribute the Leaf Record Sheet (page 29) to each group and have students gather information about the tree. Students can make bark rubbings, collect fallen leaves, etc. After returning to class, each group should glue its materials to construction paper. Have each student look at field guides, encyclopedias, etc., to find the name of her trees and write it at the bottom of the collage. Glue the record sheets to the backs of the collages. Punch two holes along the left side of the collage and bind the pages into a book with a cardboard cover. Tie the book with raffia to create a class field guide. Let students observe their trees throughout the year and compare new data to their original data.

23

SQUIRRELS AND ACORNS

Did You Know?

- Because plants do not grow in cold areas in the winter, squirrels collect nuts and store food.

- Squirrels do not hibernate, so during autumn, a squirrel's fur, including the tail, grows thicker and warmer in order to protect the squirrel from the cold.

- Squirrels' winter nests can be holes in tree trunks padded with leaves, grasses, bark, etc.

Literature Selection
Squirrels
by Brian Wildsmith: Oxford University Press, 1987. (Picture book, 32 pg.) Colorful illustrations depict the life of a busy squirrel.

Literature Selection
Sara Squirrel and the Lost Acorns
by Julie Sykes: Little Tiger Press, 1996. (Picture book, 32 pg.) Sara Squirrel agrees to bring something back for her friends after searching for acorns.

Literature Selection
A Tale of Squirrel Nutkin
by Beatrix Potter: Dover Publications, 1984. (Picture book, 32 pg.) Squirrel Nutkin bothers an owl instead of collecting nuts like other squirrels.

Be a Squirrel, Plant an Acorn

Just like trees, squirrels store food for the winter. Sometimes squirrels bury acorns and later forget where they buried them! These forgotten acorns have a good chance of sprouting in the spring and growing into oak trees. To germinate an acorn, place it, along with a wet paper towel inside a resealable plastic bag and put the bag on a sunny window sill. The acorns should sprout into two shoots. Have each student fill a cup with dirt and plant one shoot in the dirt and leave the other above ground. Watch the sprouts grow into saplings. Encourage students to take care of their saplings and plant them outdoors, if possible, in the spring.

Where Did I Hide Those Nuts?

Tammy Squirrel needs help finding some acorns she hid! Take students on an acorn hunt by copying 5-10 acorn patterns (page 30). Write a clue on each pattern, telling where the acorn is, for example, *Where people jump and run and leap, an acorn you will find to keep,* might be a clue for the gym. Put the first clue in the classroom and hide the rest around the school. Let students read the first clue and start the acorn hunt! Lead students on a walk around the school being as quiet as little squirrels. When an acorn is found, let a student read the next clue and continue on the hunt until the last acorn is found. On the last acorn, write a thank you from Tammy Squirrel and instructions to return to class for *Acorn Snacks* (page 25).

Portable Squirrel Blanket

Make blankets for squirrels! In winter, squirrels often wrap their tails around themselves like blankets to stay warm. Give each student a copy of the sleeping squirrel pattern (page 31). Provide scraps of material such as fake fur, felt, and prints, along with several tail patterns (page 31). Let students color or paint their squirrels, then cut out a tail from the fabric of their choice. Have students glue their tail blankets over the squirrels, so that the sleeping squirrels are peeking out from behind the blankets. Students can glue the completed squirrels to construction paper and draw in backgrounds for the squirrels.

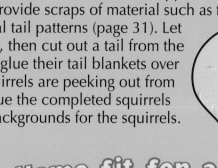

A Home fit for a Squirrel

Students can build creativity with this squirrel nest-building art project. Give each student two sheets of brown construction paper in different shades and instruct them to cut triangular notches randomly around the edges and draw in a brown wood grain pattern. Cut out a large oval in the middle of the paper and glue onto a black piece of construction paper, to create a tree hole. Cut out a rounded square shape from a different shade of brown paper and draw a squirrel face on it. Cut out and glue on a neck and ears. Glue the squirrel into the tree hole so that he is peeking out. Make fall leaves and acorns to glue on the pictures. Display the artwork on a bulletin board titled *Peeking Into Autumn*.

Go nuts over Acorn Snacks!

Students will want to squirrel away these acorn-shaped goodies. Gather one chocolate sandwich cookie for every two students, one large marshmallow for each student, and a 12-ounce bag of chocolate chips. Melt the chocolate chips in a microwave. Then, dip the marshmallows in melted chocolate and place them on their sides on waxed paper. Have students place cookie halves on the tops of chocolate-covered marshmallows to resemble acorns. Allow the "acorns" to harden and let your little "squirrels" gobble them up!

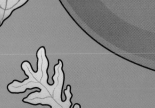

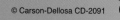

Scarecrows

Did You Know?

- The Greeks erected wooden statues of Priapus in their fields, a god who protected wheat fields and vineyards.
- Japanese scarecrows were called *kakashi* (ka•KOSH•e) and consisted of anything from bad smelling rags and fish bones to bits of shiny glass and metal.
- In medieval England, boys guarded fields by throwing rocks, shouting, and clapping wooden boards. They also used scarecrows made of sacks stuffed with straw.
- Some Native American tribes shouted at birds from platforms around the edges of the fields.

- Pennsylvania Dutch scarecrows were called *bootzamon* and *bootzafraw*, or *bogeyman* and *bogeywife*. Their heads were made from a broom or a cloth bag stuffed with straw and their bodies were made from old clothes, usually overalls, stuffed with straw.
- Today, many farmers use whirligigs, pie pans strung from posts, spotlights, and recorded sounds to scare animals or crows away, but most still have stuffed scarecrows standing in their fields.

Literature Selections

Scarecrow by Cynthia Rylant: Harcourt Brace, 1998. (Picture book, 40 pg.) A scarecrow enjoys his work and actually likes birds!

Scarecrow! by Valerie Littlewood: Penguin Putnam Books, 1995. (Children's reference book, 32 pg.) Details the history of scarecrows with beautiful illustrations.

Scarecrow Friend

Scare up a real masterpiece with this life-size scarecrow. Provide old pants, a long-sleeved shirt, trash bag, straw hat, hay or straw, a paper grocery sack, markers, crayons, and newspaper. Have students work together to construct a scarecrow. To make the scarecrow's body, stuff the trash bag with crumpled newspaper and place it inside the shirt. Tuck the shirt into the waist of the pants. Stuff the arms and legs with crumpled newspaper and stick straw or hay out of the ends. To make the head, turn a paper grocery sack inside out. Draw a face on the sack and stuff it with newspaper. Place the head in the shirt, then top it with the hat. Place straw around the neck and at the waist to complete the scarecrow. Position the scarecrow on a chair or on a bale of hay beside a basket of fall reading selections and let students read to the scarecrow.

Falling Into Autumn

The Face of a Scarecrow

Make scarecrow masks with this art project. Give each student a paper plate, scissors, glue, crayons, straw, buttons, and a hat pattern (page 31). Cut out eye and mouth holes and let students color their masks to look like scarecrow faces, with button noses. Let each student decorate and cut out his hat pattern and glue it to the top of the mask. Glue bits of straw on the plate to finish. Measure a length of elastic to fit around each child's head and tape it to the mask.

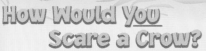

How Would You Scare a Crow?

What do fish bones and pie pans have in common? They can both be used to scare crows! Talk about the history of scarecrows around the world (see *Did You Know?* information on page 26). Provide large pieces of construction paper, scraps of fabric, straw, foil, sequins, etc., and challenge students to create a scarecrow with elements used by farmers around the world, including shiny objects, human-shaped figures, etc. Let students assemble their scarecrows on paper and draw in extra details and a background. Let each student point out the features of her scarecrow to the class.

Scarecrow Puppet

Make scarecrow puppets to keep the crows away. Copy the scarecrow patterns (page 32) for each student. Have students color and cut out each piece. Provide straw, cloth scraps, ribbon, wiggly eyes, ric-rac, etc., for students to decorate the scarecrows. Punch holes as indicated on the scarecrow. Provide brads and let students connect the pieces to make the scarecrow. Glue a craft stick to the back of the scarecrow to make a puppet. Students can use the completed puppet to create a scarecrow skit.

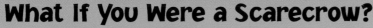

What If You Were a Scarecrow?

Have students put themselves in a scarecrow's shoes, (or hay!). Ask students to brainstorm what a scarecrow might think about all day. All of the animals are scared of him, the farmer never stops to talk, and he can't move from his post! Have students write an article for a magazine on the life of a scarecrow, written from the scarecrow's point of view. Challenge students to come up with catchy titles for their articles, such as *Scarecrow Speaks Out* or *Tired of Scaring!* Display the completed articles near the *Scarecrow Friend* (page 26).

27

© Carson-Dellosa CD-2091

Celebrate Autumn

Treat your students to a fall party. Let them sing the song below, wear their scarecrow masks (page 27), share their fall leaf artwork and writing, perform skits with their scarecrow puppets (page 27), and snack on acorn snacks (page 25) and haystacks (see right)!

Haystacks

Serve these fall treats at your autumn celebration. To make haystacks, gather 2 packages of butterscotch chips, 1 large package of chow mein noodles and sunflower seeds (optional). Melt the chips in a heavy pan over low heat. Remove from heat, add noodles, and stir until coated. Drop by tablespoons onto waxed paper and refrigerate to cool. Serve the haystacks with apple cider for a fall feast!

What We See in Autumn

(sing to the tune of *Skip to My Lou*)

Divide the class into four groups. Have the first group sing the chorus between verses, at the beginning, and at the end. Have the other three groups sing and act out the verses.

Chorus:
See, see, what do you see? See, see, what do you see?
See, see, what do you see?
What do you see in autumn?
(Students put hands above eyes, as if looking at a distance.)

First Verse:
Scarecrow in the cornfield, shoo crow shoo.
Scarecrow in the cornfield, shoo crow shoo.
Scarecrow in the cornfield, shoo crow shoo.
That's what we see in autumn.
(Students act like scarecrows, shooing crows away.)

Second Verse:
Squirrels hiding acorns, run squirrels run.
Squirrels hiding acorns, run squirrels run.
Squirrels hiding acorns, run squirrels run.
That's what we see in autumn.
(Students run around and pretend to hide acorns.)

Third Verse:
Leaves in bright colors, fall leaves fall.
Leaves in bright colors, fall leaves fall.
Leaves in bright colors, fall leaves fall.
That's what we see in autumn.
(Students put hands to sides and wiggle fingers, as they bring hands to ground.)

Leaf Record Sheet

Name_____

Class _____

Date_____

Season_____

Where is your tree located? _____

How big around is your tree's trunk? _____ inches. (This number should match the approximate age of your tree.)

How old do you think your tree is? _____ years old.

How tall is your tree? _____ feet tall.

How does the bark on the tree look and feel? _____

What color or colors are the leaves? _____

What shape are the leaves? _____

Write about any special features on your tree, such as nests, animals, or scars on the leaves or bark.

_____

_____

_____

Draw seeds, flowers or other things on your tree in the space below.

Bonus Activity–Have someone take a picture of you this year beside your tree. Try to have your picture taken in October for as many years as possible. Watch you and your tree grow!

deciduous tree

evergreen tree

acorn
(also use with bulletin board idea pg. 14)

squirrel
(use with bulletin board idea pg. 14)

30

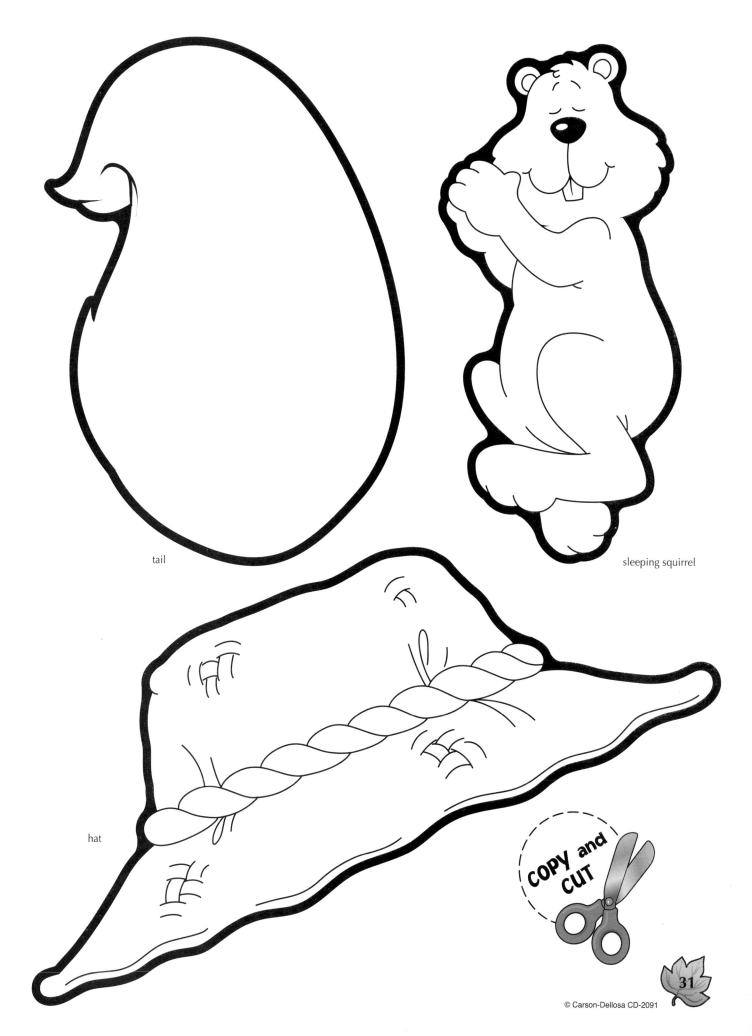

tail

sleeping squirrel

hat

COPY and CUT

31

© Carson-Dellosa CD-2091

scarecrow
(also use with bulletin board idea pg. 14)

COPY and CUT

leaves

32

© Carson-Dellosa CD-2091

A HARVEST OF AUTUMN BOOKS

A Tree Is Nice

by Janice May Udry
HarperCollins Children's Books, 1981
(Picture book, 32 pages)

This Caldecott Medal winner describes all the good things trees do for people, from providing shade to producing apples.

A Tree Is Fun Promote tree appreciation by having children illustrate the ways trees make people's lives more enjoyable. Share *A Tree Is Nice* with the class and talk about the different ways trees are used in the illustrations. Give each child an 11" x 17" piece of white construction paper. Using watercolors, have each student paint a tree trunk with branches and fall leaves. After the paint is dry, provide crayons and markers and have students illustrate different things that can be done in, under, or with a tree. Ideas include swinging on a tree swing, building a treehouse, or resting under the shade of a tree. Display the completed trees to create a forest of fall fun.

Award Winner

33

Red Leaf, Yellow Leaf

by Lois Ehlert
Harcourt Brace & Company
1991. (Picture book, 36 pages)

A child shares a scrapbook describing the life cycle of a maple tree from a seed to a tree, then shares a favorite leaf from the tree.

A Leaf Tells All Each student can speak from the point of view of a leaf with this activity. Let each child create a small booklet by giving her a half sheet of construction paper to fold and staple into a booklet. Have each child find one fall leaf outside, attach the leaf to the cover of her booklet, and write a title under it. On the booklet pages, have students write and illustrate how the leaf sprouts from a bud, how it grows, how it changes color, how it falls in autumn, and how it might feel going through these changes.

Pumpkin Fiesta

by Caryn Yacowitz: HarperCollins Publishers, 1998
(Picture book, 32 pages)

Old Juana always grows the best pumpkins and wins a special crown each year. Foolish Fernando decides he can grow better pumpkins than Old Juana and thinks he has figured out her secret. When Fernando lazily follows the steps, he discovers there is much more to Old Juana's technique than he thought.

Hard Work Pays Off Help students understand the benefits of hard work. Talk about how Old Juana worked hard to help her pumpkins grow and how Foolish Fernando took shortcuts and skipped important steps. Share and explain the saying *Reap what you sow*. For example, Old Juana sprinkled three seeds per mound; Fernando threw the seeds in all directions. Old Juana watered each plant; Foolish Fernando threw water on some plants, not on all, etc. Have the children think of things they do that require hard work. Have each student fold a piece of paper in half. On the first half, they can write and illustrate the hard work they had to do. On the opposite half, they can write and illustrate how the work paid off. For example, *I practiced the flute every night* and *I played well enough to be in the spring concert*.

The Biggest Pumpkin Ever

by Steven Kroll
Holiday House, 1984
(Picture book, 32 pages)

Two field mice find the same pumpkin in a garden, but each has different plans for it. One mouse wants to enter the pumpkin in the town contest and the other wants to carve it into a jack-o'-lantern. Eventually they find a solution that pleases them both.

My Pumpkin Is… Your class will enjoy these silly pumpkin similes. First, have students describe the size of the pumpkin from *The Biggest Pumpkin Ever* by comparing it to another object. Then, have them write their comparisons on construction paper. Next, turn the paper over and illustrate the descriptions by combining the object and the pumpkin into one item. Divide the class into groups and let them show their pictures and have their classmates guess the objects.

When the Frost Is on the Punkin

by James Whitcomb Riley
David R. Godine, Publisher, Inc., 1991
(Picture book, 32 pages)
A child enjoys an autumn morning on a farm. The text is a classic read-aloud poem celebrating autumn changes.

Sounds of Autumn Explain that the poem featured in *When the Frost is on the Punkin* uses words to describe sounds. Some of the words are familiar sound words, such as *buzzin', clackin',* and *cluckin'.* Other words, such as *kyouck* and *hallylooyer,* were written by the author to describe the sounds of turkeys and roosters. Have the children write 4-5 line poems about the changing seasons. Challenge them to make up new words that describe the sounds in their poems.

Different Dialects Read the story to the children, explaining that the poet wrote in a Midwestern dialect. Talk about how people in different regions of a country may pronounce words in different ways. As you read the story aloud, have the children point out words that are spelled as they are pronounced. Examples include *punkin* for pumpkin, *tossels* for tassels, and *airly* for early. Let students take turns reading lines from the poem as it is written, then again pronouncing the words in their own dialect.

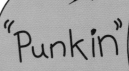
"Punkin"

35

The Ghost-Eye Tree

by Bill Martin, Jr. and John Archambault
Holt, Henry & Co., 1988. (Picture book, 32 pages)

One autumn night, a boy and his sister must get a bucket of milk for their mother. Their journey takes them past the dreaded ghost-eye tree, where their imaginations run wild.

Not What It Looks Like Sometimes things are not what they seem! Explain that in the story, the children think the tree comes alive, when in reality, the knots in its trunk, the wind through its branches, and the childrens' imaginations made the tree appear to be alive. Encourage students to think of times when their imaginations made them afraid of things that would normally not frighten them. Give each child a piece of construction paper. Have her turn the paper vertically and fold the top halfway down and the bottom halfway up. On the folded paper, instruct students to illustrate something that looks scary at night, but not during the day. Then, have students open their papers and draw pictures of what the objects actually are during the day. On the front, have each student complete the sentence *I thought it was a _____* . On the inside, have him complete the sentence, *But it was only a _____*. Older children can write short stories about their objects. Let students share the completed projects with their classmates.

Possum's Harvest Moon

by Anne Hunter
Houghton Mifflin Company, 1998
(Picture book, 32 pages)

When Possum wakes up one autumn night and sees the bright harvest moon, he decides to have a moonlight party for his forest friends. As he visits each friend, he discovers that everyone is too busy getting ready for winter to join the party.

A Moonlight Party Create shimmering moonlight invitations for a class party! Talk with students about the night animals featured in the story, such as the opossum, raccoons, fireflies, etc. Have the class choose an animal to host a harvest moon party. Encourage them to think about what food to serve at the party and what the entertainment might be. Have them think of a fun name for the party and let each student make an invitation. Give each child a half sheet of black paper and a white or yellow crayon and have him draw a circle at the top to resemble a moon. Use the empty space on the invitation to write about the party. After the invitation is complete, students can sprinkle gold glitter on the moon to create a shimmering effect. Then, have a class moonlight party! Serve moon cupcakes (chocolate cupcakes sprinkled with confectioner's sugar) and sparkling star juice (powdered lemonade mixed with sparkling water).

36

The Little Scarecrow Boy

by Margaret Wise Brown
HarperCollins Juvenile Books, 1998
(Picture book, 40 pages)

A scarecrow boy wants to help his father in the cornfield, but his father tells him he does not look fierce enough to scare a crow. After much practice, the boy sneaks into the cornfield and musters all of his scary faces to keep the crows away.

Scary Scarecrow Faces Let students show how scary they can be by making fierce faces like the little scarecrow boy in the story. Then, take a close-up instant photograph of each child making his scariest face or have the student draw a picture of himself making a scary face. Cut out the faces and glue each to the center of a piece of construction paper. Provide crayons, markers, wallpaper, and fabric scraps. Let students make hats (students can use the hat pattern on page 31) and shirts and glue them to their face pictures to complete the scarecrows. Provide pieces of straw for decorating, as well. Display the scarecrows and have your class and other classes vote to determine which student is the scariest scarecrow.

Jeb Scarecrow's Pumpkin Patch

by Jana Dillon
Houghton Mifflin Company, 1992
(Picture book, 32 pages)

A conscientious scarecrow watches over his family's pumpkin patch, guarding it from hungry crows. When he finds out the crows are planning to hold their harvest celebration in his pumpkin patch, he must think of ways to keep his pumpkins safe.

Pumpkin Disguises Read *Jeb Scarecrow's Pumpkin Patch* and talk about how Jeb disguised his pumpkins as jack-o'-lanterns to frighten the crows. Children can draw or trace a pumpkin shape onto orange paper. Have them decorate one side like a pumpkin and the other side like a jack-o'-lantern by outlining the features using neon-colored craft glue. Next, cut out and glue the pumpkin to a wooden craft stick. Reread the story. When the pumpkin patch is mentioned in the book, have each child hold up the pumpkin side of his completed craft. When the crows enter the pumpkin patch, have him hold up the jack-o'-lantern side and make scary noises.

37

Fired Up About... FIRE SAFETY

Spark students' knowledge of fire prevention and safety with these hot ideas! Students will learn about everything from exiting buildings and inspecting their homes to making arts and crafts that emphasize fire safety.

Did You Know?

🔥 National Fire Prevention Week occurs during the week of October 9.

🔥 On October 9, 1871, in the city of Chicago, a spectacular fire was a disaster for the city and its residents. This fire, known as the Great Chicago Fire, is famous not only because it brought about improvements in fire prevention and safety procedures, but also because of the legend regarding the fire's origin. According to legend, while Mrs. Catherine O'Leary of Chicago was milking her cow, the cow kicked over an oil lamp, setting Mrs. O'Leary's barn on fire and starting the fire that burned through the city.

Literature Selections

🔥 *I'm a Fire Fighter* by Mary Packard: Scholastic, Inc., 1995. (Picture book, 32 pg.) A boy pretends to be a firefighter who saves a cat.

🔥 *A Trip to the Firehouse* by Wendy Cheyette Lewiston: Putnam Publishing Group, 1998. (Picture book, 32 pg.) Action photos depict a day in the life of a firefighter.

🔥 *Big Frank's Fire Truck* by Leslie McGuire: Random House, 1996. (Picture book, 32 pg.) Frank's crew answers emergency calls and more!

🔥 *It's a Fire Drill Day!* (Dinofours) by Steve Metzger: Scholastic, 1997. (Picture book, 32 pg.) A dinosaur is afraid on fire drill day at school.

Stop Drop & Roll

What Mrs. O'Leary's Cow Said

Learn how much your class already knows about fire safety. Have each student draw or paint Mrs. O'Leary's cow, then add speech balloons with fire safety tips written inside the balloons. Allow older students to create a fire safety cartoon starring Mrs. O'Leary's cow. Post the illustrations on a bulletin board titled *Fire Safety Tips from Mrs. O'Leary's Cow*.

INTERVIEW A FIREFIGHTER

To kick off your study of fire safety, invite a local firefighter to class or arrange to visit a local fire station. Brainstorm a list of interview questions. If a visit is not possible, have students compose letters asking their questions and send them to a local fire station. Then, read the responses in class.

Home Fire Safety Inspections

Students can become junior fire inspectors with this safety exercise. Explain that public buildings, including schools, are routinely inspected for fire hazards, such as materials placed near hot spots, fire alarms or extinguishers that do not work properly, or blocked exits. Explain that inspections should also take place at home. Reproduce a Fire Safety Inspector Worksheet (page 45) for students to take home, and ask that adults help them complete it. Explain that if a situation at home does not match the safe practices pictured on the worksheet, they should ask an adult to fix the situation so that their home is free of fire hazards.

Thank You, Firefighters

After visiting with local firefighters, design red-hot thank you cards to send to your local fire station. For younger students, reproduce fire hat patterns (page 47) and have them write on the patterns. Older students can work together to design a giant fire truck card on red bulletin board paper. Discuss elements of a letter, such as greeting, body, and closure, and then have everyone write a thank you letter on the giant card.

39

Be a Firefighter

Dress your students in firefighter badges and hats to reward them for making sure their homes are safe. Each student should mount a fire safety badge pattern (page 47) copied on red paper onto tagboard and trim. Then, dot the badges with glue and sprinkle with red glitter. Attach the badges to the new "firefighters'" shirts. Then, enlarge fire hat patterns (page 47) on red construction paper. Cut out and decorate the hats. To make the hats wearable, glue each fire hat pattern to the front of a 5"–wide paper headband.

FIRE SAFETY INSPECTOR

Bucket Brigade Teamwork

Learn a little fire fighting history with this game. Explain that fire fighting has changed over the years. Before there were fire hydrants, firefighters used buckets to fetch water from wells or streams. Teamwork was an essential part of this firefighting technique as lines of firefighters passed buckets to a *thrower* who tossed the water on the fire. To have an outside bucket brigade relay, gather two large buckets, two small pails, and one large tub of water (use sand or confetti for a dry relay). Divide the class into two teams and have them line up at an arm's length from each other. Position the tub of water between the two teams and place a large bucket behind each team's line. Explain that the first person in each line will be given a small pail, and should (on signal) go to the large tub, fill the pail, and pass the pail down the line. When the bucket reaches the last person in line, pour the contents into the large bucket, and pass the bucket back down the line to be refilled. The first team to fill its large bucket is the winner.

REMINDER
Change the batteries in your smoke detectors.

What's That Sound?

This "alarming" activity will prepare students for fire safety. Explain that smoke detectors sound an alarm when smoke or extreme heat is near the detector. Bring in a smoke detector and show what it looks and sounds like. Display the battery in the smoke detector and explain that eventually the battery will stop working properly. Make reminder cards about students checking their home smoke detector batteries. Give each student a copy of the battery pattern (page 47) to glue onto a piece of tagboard and then cut out. Let each student color the battery and sign her name at the bottom of the letter. Send the reminder cards to parents.

Emergency Numbers
Fire 555-4321
Police 555-9876
Poison 555-7654

EMERGENCY MAGNETS

Turn important information and phone numbers into handy, decorative magnets. Give each student tagboard, markers, and emergency phone numbers for the fire station, police station, and poison control office in your area. Write the names and phone numbers on the tagboard and decorate the border. Laminate the completed tagboard and attach magnet tape to the back. Send the magnets home for display near a telephone.

What Would You Say in an Emergency?

Practice emergency phone conversations with real phones. Provide a disconnected telephone for the class to use to practice what they should say in an emergency. Explain that it is important for them to know their addresses, phone numbers, and parents' names in case of an emergency. Discuss how emergency phone numbers should only be called in true emergencies and that if the emergency is a fire, people in the house or building should exit immediately and call from another location (such as a neighbor's house). Allow each child to use the class phone to dial the emergency number to the fire station and tell his name, address, phone number, and parents' names. Have another student play the role of the operator to prompt the students for information. Display a completed Emergency Magnet (see activity above) to aid students in the activity.

HOT Door COOL Door

Junior fire chiefs can learn a new fire emergency tip with this game. Explain that in a fire, students should always check the temperature of a door by feeling it before they open it. If a door is hot, fire is behind the door, making it unsafe to open. If a door is cool or room temperature, fire is probably not outside the door, making it safe to open slowly. Teach this concept by having a student "Fire Chief" stand on the far side of a room, and have the class stand at the opposite side. Have the Chief turn her back to the others and call out "Cool Door!" Students should begin walking towards her. If the Chief calls out "Hot Door!" and turns around, everyone should freeze in position. If the Chief sees anyone moving, she should send that classmate back to the starting line. The first student to reach the Chief becomes the Chief for the next game.

41

STOP, DROP, & ROLL

Explain the *Stop, Drop, and Roll* technique for smothering fire on burning clothing with this inter- active activity. Ask students if they know what oxygen is. Not only must humans and animals breath oxygen to stay alive, but fires also need it to keep burning. Explain that one method of fire extinguishing is smothering the fire with materials that do not allow the fire to receive oxygen. Tell them that if their clothes catch on fire, they should *Stop* where they are, *Drop*

to the ground, and *Roll* back and forth so that the fire will be smothered. Invite one student to demonstrate the Stop, Drop, and Roll method and then allow everyone to practice outside or in an open area. Photo- graph each child demonstrating the Stop, Drop, and Roll technique and display the pictures on a bulletin board titled *We Can Stop, Drop, and Roll!*

TIMELY EXITS

Teach students that timing is everything when leaving a burning building. If the class has practiced a fire drill at school, have them recall the rules for the fire drill and where they should meet outside. Have them explain the importance of walking in a quiet, or- derly manner and exiting quickly, yet safely. Conduct a class fire drill and use a stopwatch to time how long it takes the class to line up, exit the classroom and building, and arrive at their destination in a quiet and orderly manner. Record the time. After several fire drills, use the data to make a line graph to see if time was improved. Older students can use the data to find the average time it takes the class to complete a fire drill.

GO!

Get Out & Stay Out!

"Get Out and Stay Out!" is an important fire safety rule. If a building is on fire, leave the building (Get Out!) and do not return for anything (Stay Out!). Just as school fire drills prepare students for a fire emergency, every family needs a *Get Out and Stay Out* plan in case of a fire at home. Have each student draw a map of his home. Explain that fire escape plans need two exits in case one is blocked by fire. Then, have students draw two exit routes from each room in the house. After the exits are marked on the map, have them mark a specific location away from the house where the family can meet. Send their escape plans home to be shared with their families. After a few days, discuss how families have planned for exiting their houses and meeting at designated places.

Fire Escape Plan

42

Fire Safety Booklets

Students can share fire safety tips at home with reference booklets. Reproduce a Fire Safety Booklet (page 46) for each student. Direct students to use the word bank at the top of page 46 to complete each sentence, then illustrate the sentences. When the pages are finished, discuss which words complete each sentence. Then, cut out the pages and staple them together to make booklets. Allow students to take home their booklets and share them with their families.

Extinguishing Art

Make fire safety creative by making pretend fire extinguishers. Explain that fire prevention experts recommend that extinguishers be placed in areas of a house where there is the potential for fire, such as the kitchen or garage. Most extinguishers contain special foam that smothers oxygen in the fire, causing it to go out. Before beginning this project, take students on a tour of the school and point out fire extinguishers. Provide clean, plastic soda bottles. Direct students to paint the bottles red. (Tip: Add a few drops of liquid starch to the paint so the paint will stick to the plastic.) Tie one end of a 12" piece of thick yarn around the neck of the bottle. Then, squeeze glue onto the top of the cap and place a large craft stick horizontally across the cap to represent the handle of the fire extinguisher.

MATERIALS

- 2-liter drink bottle
- Thick yarn
- Craft stick
- Red paint
- Brushes
- Liquid starch

Smoke Crawl

Learn how to avoid smoke with this low-crawling game! Discuss how inhaling too much smoke or toxic gas from a fire can be as deadly as the fire itself. Fire safety experts recommend crawling low to the ground if there is ever a need to vacate a house due to a fire. Because smoke rises, the area close to the floor should have less smoke than the area at standing level. To play "Smoke Crawl," a game similar to limbo, have four students hold the corners of an open bedsheet and have the other students crawl under the sheet without touching it. Lower the sheet each time the group has made it through. Reward the student who is able to crawl closest to the ground without touching the sheet.

43

Fire Safety

Fire Safety
(Sing to the tune of *B-I-N-G-O*)

Have students pretend to punch buttons on a phone.
If there's a fire in my house, this is what I'll do,
Get out and stay out. Get out and stay out.
Get out and stay out, and then call 9-1-1.

Have students roll on the ground.
If my clothes should catch on fire, this is what I'll do.
Stop, drop, and roll around. Stop, drop, and roll around.
Stop, drop, and roll around. This is what I'll do.

Have students crawl on the ground.
If smoke makes it hard to breathe, this is what I'll do.
Crawl close to the ground. Crawl close to the ground.
Crawl close to the ground. This is what I'll do.

Have students point to the door.
When I get out of my house, this is where I'll go,
To our meeting place. To our meeting place.
To our meeting place. This is where I'll go.

Dalmatian Puppets

Dalmatians have been the unofficial mascots for fire stations and fire prevention agencies for years. In the early days of fire fighting, dalmatians were used by firefighters to guard fire wagons and hoses. Dalmatians were often used to coach horses who were pulling fire wagons into running at a faster pace. To celebrate the dalmatian firehouse mascot, make dalmatian sock puppets. Provide a class supply of clean, white, adult-size athletic socks. Cut strips of poster board the same width and length as the socks and put the socks over the poster board. Glue two wiggly eyes on the sock to be the dog's eyes. Dip a sponge or cotton ball into black paint and use the paint to make black spots, a nose, and black ears on the puppet. Tie red ribbon around the puppets' necks for collars. Let students use their dalmatian puppets to recite a fire safety rule to the class.

Fire Safety Inspector Worksheet

Smoke Detectors

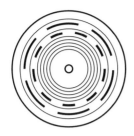

❑ Batteries in all smoke detectors are working.

Sockets with two Plugs

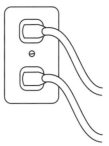

❑ Electrical outlets are not overloaded.

Extension Cords

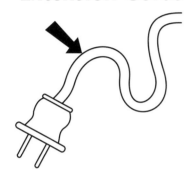

❑ Covering on extension cords is in good condition.

Cleaning Bottles

❑ Chemicals and cleaners are stored away from heat and flames.

Matches and Lighters

❑ Matches and lighters are safely stored.

Newspapers and Magazines

❑ Papers and magazines are neatly stored away from any heat source.

We have inspected our home for the above fire safety practices.

Adult _____

Student _____

Fire Safety Booklet

Use the words in the word bank to complete the sentences below. Then, draw a picture to match each sentence. In the first box, draw a fire safety cover. Cut the pages out and staple the pages together to make a Fire Safety Booklet.

Word Bank: stay cool meeting get smoke roll exit low hot

Name _____

Always have two ways to _____ a building in case of a fire, and have a designated _____ place.

If a closed door feels _____ , do not open it. If the door is _____ , it is okay to open.

Crawl _____ to the ground to avoid breathing in _____ from the fire.

Remember to "stop, drop, and _____ " if your clothes ever catch on fire.

The first thing you should do if you are in a building that is on fire is "_____ out and _____ out!"

46

COPY and CUT

FD

fire hat

battery

FIRE SAFETY INSPECTOR

fire safety badge

magnifying glass
(use with bulletin board idea pg. 15)

47

© Carson-Dellosa CD-2091

In 1492... Columbus Day

Set sail for success with these Columbus Day activities. Students will explore Columbus, his voyage, and his times through activities in dramatic play, language arts, crafts, map-making, and much more! Gather your provisions and prepare for an exciting journey into the past!

Did You Know?

- ✷ Christopher Columbus and most educated people of his time thought the earth was shaped like a sphere, not flat.

- ✷ Columbus's voyage was sponsored by King Ferdinand and Queen Isabella of Spain in return for spices, gold, and silks he would bring back from China.

- ✷ Columbus set sail on August 3, 1492, from Spain with three ships, the Santa Maria, Niña, and Pinta.

- ✷ On October 12, 1492, Columbus landed on an island in the Bahamas, which he believed was the East Indies. He also explored other islands, including Cuba and Hispaniola.

- ✷ Columbus brought gold, jewels, pineapples, and even parrots back from his voyage!

- ✷ On his return to Spain, Columbus was hailed as a hero and was given the title *Admiral of the Ocean Seas*.

- ✷ Columbus died in 1506, still believing he had reached China.

Literature Selections

I, Columbus—My Journal 1492-3 by Peter and Connie Roop: Walker & Company, 1990. (Chapter book, 57 pg.) Contains translated passages from Columbus's actual journal.

In 1492 by Jean Marzollo: Scholastic, 1991. (Picture book, 40 pg.) Rhyming text tells the story of Columbus's voyage.

The Niña, Pinta, and the Santa Maria by Dennis Brindell Fradin: Franklin Watts, 1991. (Chapter book, 64 pg.) This biography focuses on Columbus's voyage to the new world.

A Picture Book of Christopher Columbus by David Adler: Holiday House, 1992. (Picture book, 32 pg.) Presents Columbus's life and voyages.

Christopher Columbus

Where in the World is Christopher Columbus?

Columbus thought he could sail west to get to the east! To show students why he thought this, trace an imaginary line from Spain, east to China, on a globe. Have students point out obstacles along the way. Columbus studied geography maps and books before his voyages, but since no one knew that North and South America existed, he thought his path west would be clear.

How Do I Get There?

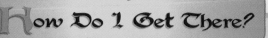

Students can tell you how to get there by making maps. Explain that people of Columbus's time, including map makers (called cartographers), often used a type of paper called parchment. Parchment was rough and brownish-yellow, and originally made from animal skins. To make "parchment," give each student a large piece of brown paper grocery bag. Crumple the bags several times, making the paper soft and worn. Have younger students draw maps from the classroom to the playground. Instruct older students to use a present day map to draw Spain and Portugal on the right side of their papers and the Caribbean Islands on the left. Draw lines connecting the two locations. Have students add details to their maps, such as ships, a compass rose, etc. If desired, students can glue wooden dowel rods on each end of their map and roll each end inward towards the center, forming a scroll.

Join Christopher Columbus on

The Adventure of a Lifetime!

Because many sailors thought the world was flat and feared sea monsters and other unknowns, Columbus had to convince them to come on the voyage. Discuss persuasive writing and have students design posters to convince sailors to join Christopher Columbus's voyage. Encourage children to think of slogans and artwork that might persuade sailors to join Columbus on the trip.

Sailing with Columbus

Have students sail away with Columbus by writing journal entries. Have the class brainstorm adjectives or phrases which describe the fears and excitement Columbus's crew may have felt both before and during the journey and list them on the board. Have students write two journal entries from the point of view of a crew member or Columbus. Instruct students to date one entry August 3, 1492, (the date Columbus and his crew departed from Spain) and another October 12, 1492 (the date land was sighted). Allow the children to perform dramatic readings of their entries for the class.

49

The Flat World Theory

Show students the world is round! Have students stand in a group behind you. With a globe facing the class, move a toy boat towards the students from Spain to China and then around the globe. As the boat moves, first the mast is visible, then the entire ship. Explain that two of Columbus' ships would have appeared this way to him as he was sailing, proving to him that the Earth is not flat. To show the flat world theory, place the same boat on a flat surface. As the boat moves, the entire object is visible, but appears smaller.

I'm Going on a Sea Voyage and I'll Take...

Before his voyage, Columbus decided who would travel with him. Next, he decided what food to bring. Because there was no refrigeration on the ship, he chose items that would not spoil, such as cheese, dried fruit, beans, and salted meats and fish. Finally, he chose personal belongings that would not take up much space. He took his journal, a special flag to fly when he reached land, and some glass beads and trinkets to trade. Ask students to think about the people, foods, and special items they would take on a sea voyage and let them complete the Going on a Sea Voyage worksheet (page 55).

You Can Be Columbus

Persistence can pay off! Columbus repeated his request to the King and Queen for the funds needed to make his voyage. Have children work in small groups and assign each student a part: King Ferdinand, Queen Isabella, or Columbus. Provide props such as crowns, scarves, etc., and let each group act out a scene. Have the child playing Columbus write a reason he might give to support his voyage. Reasons might include to find gold, to find a shorter route to China, etc. Have the children playing King Ferdinand and Queen Isabella write a reason why they would not support the voyage. Reasons might include that the trip would be costly, that the ships may not find new lands, etc.

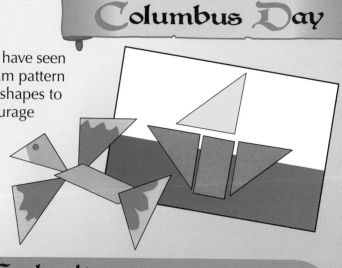

Tangram Ships or Puzzles

Use tangrams shapes to create items Columbus might have seen on his voyages. Give each child a copy of the tangram pattern (page 54). Cut out the tangram shapes, then use the shapes to create a ship, parrot, pineapple, or other item. Encourage the children to use all of the shapes in creating the pictures. Have each child glue the shapes to a piece of construction paper, color them, and create a background to complete the picture. To make puzzles, have students create scenes on the tangram patterns, cut out the patterns, and solve each others' puzzles.

New Explorations

Columbus and his crew did not know what they would find in their travels. Have students brainstorm what it might have been like for Columbus and his crew to see the Native Americans and for the Native Americans to see Columbus and his crew. Encourage children to think of places that are being explored today, such as outer space. Have students write science fiction stories, paralleling Columbus' voyage, about exploring outer space. Encourage students to name their three ships, describe the captain and the crew's fears, and detail encounters with new life forms, lands, etc. Let students write and illustrate their books. Then, have the children bind their books and include a title page and a dedication. Place the books in a learning center for other students to enjoy.

Classroom Explorers

Students can learn directions with this fun game! For younger students, label each wall of the classroom with a cardinal direction. For older students, include *northwest, northeast, southwest,* and *southeast,* as well. Divide the class into three teams and name each team Niña, Pinta, or Santa Maria. Have each team choose a child to be the explorer. Allow a member of each team to draw a card with an object in the room written on it, making sure their team's explorer does not see the card. Then, at the starting signal, have the team members give their explorers directions to find the object using directional words, for example, "Go three steps south." The first team whose explorer reaches the correct object wins the game.

69 Days at Sea

Help students imagine how long a 69 day trip would last. Make 69 copies of the ship pattern (page 53) and write the numbers 1-69 on the patterns. Pick a day and have a student post the ship numbered 1 on a wall. Continue posting the ships until you have a chain of 69. At regular intervals, discuss how students would feel if they had been travelling for that many days, and how Columbus' crew must have felt when they reached their destination. On day 69, have a New World arrival party featuring pineapple, pictures of parrots, and other items found in the new world.

Spice Scents

What's that smell? Ask students to find out! Columbus brought back many spices from his voyages, including pepper, ginger, cinnamon, and cloves. Fill several small film canisters with different spices. Number the canisters and keep a list of which spice corresponds to each number. Divide students into groups and give each group a canister. Have the children smell the spice, then tell students which spice it is. Next, have the children close their eyes, and try to identify the spices by simply smelling them. Have each group decide what spice they think is in the container and record the number on the container and their group's guess. After each group has guessed, rotate the canisters to the next group and repeat the process for the new spice. Continue rotating until each group has voted on each canister. Then, let a child from each group tell the class their group's guesses. Record the information on the board. After all the predictions have been made, tell students the correct answers and let them smell the spices again.

Columbus' Ships

Build ship crafts to celebrate exploration. Make several copies of the ship pattern (page 53) and cut them out. Give each student a piece of self-adhesive shelf paper with a wood-textured design. Trace a ship pattern on the back of the self-adhesive paper and cut out the pattern. Attach the self-adhesive paper to blue construction paper. Glue three wooden craft sticks to the top of the ship pattern as masts. Cut three squares from fabric scraps and attach one to each mast to resemble sails. Let students add details to their pictures using markers or crayons.

Niña, Pinta, Santa Maria
Sing to the tune of *Are You Sleeping?*

Niña, Pinta,
Santa Maria
Sailed away,
One fine day.
Columbus loved the sea,
But was glad to see
Land Ho! Land Ho!

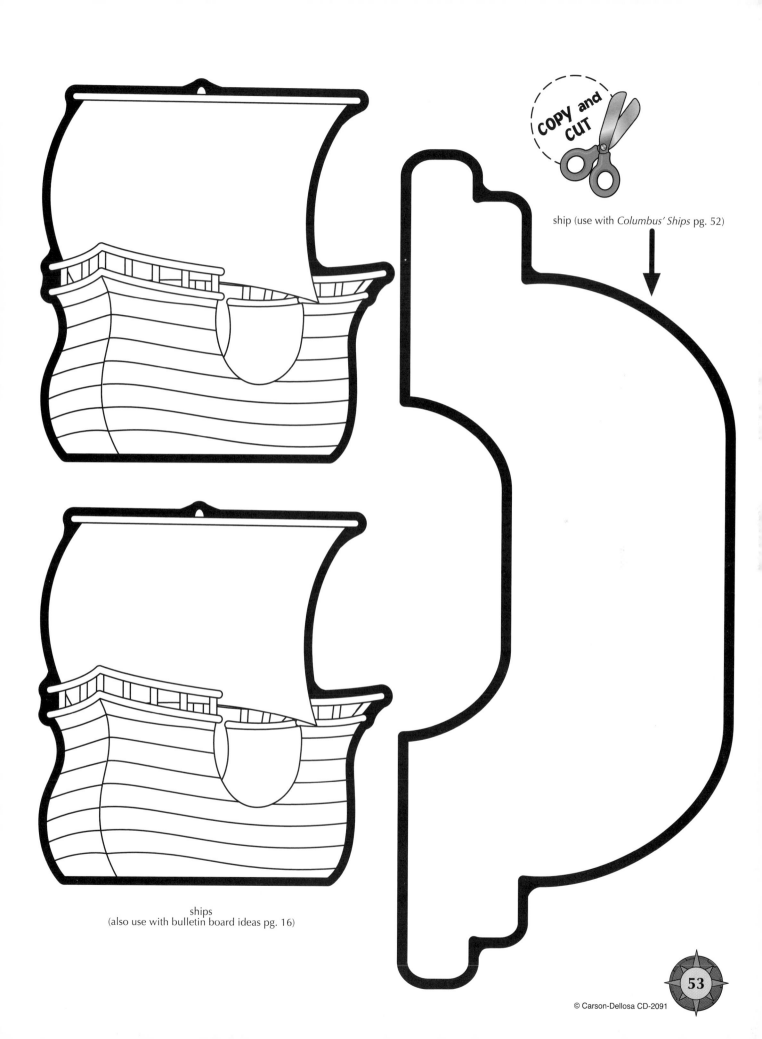

ship (use with *Columbus' Ships* pg. 52)

ships
(also use with bulletin board ideas pg. 16)

53

tangram pattern (also use with *Bat Tangram* activity pg. 88)

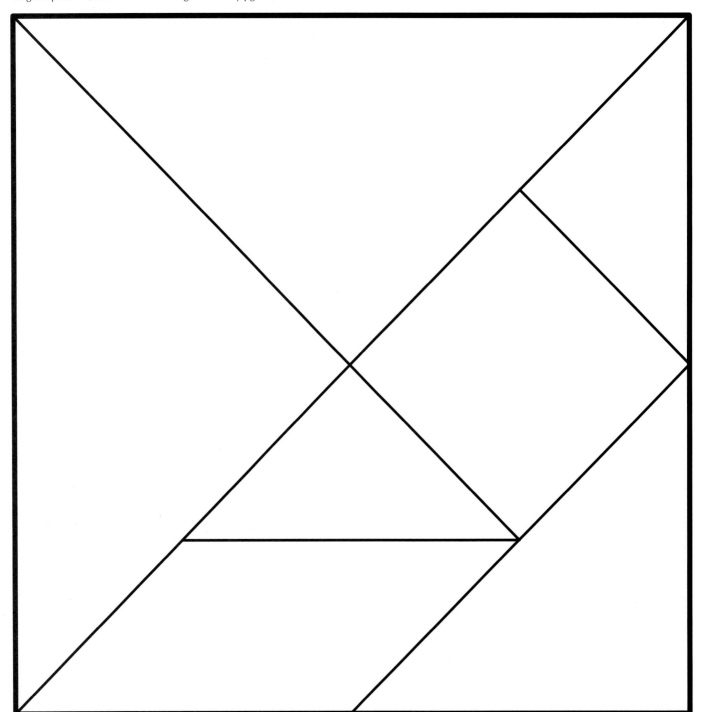

Name ______________________________

Going on a Sea Voyage

Write about a sea voyage on the lines. On a separate sheet of paper, draw the things you would take on your voyage.

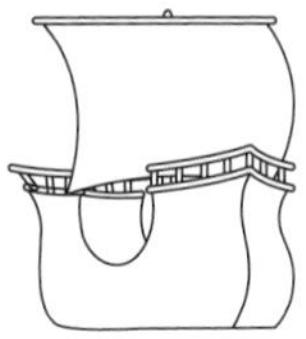

People I Would Take on a Sea Voyage

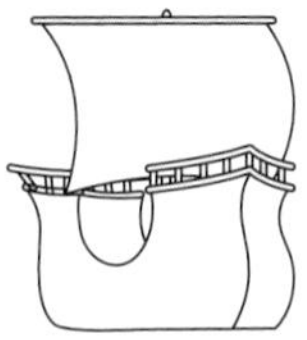

Foods I Would Take on a Sea Voyage

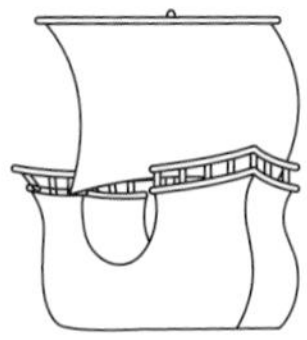

Things from Home I Would Take on a Sea Voyage

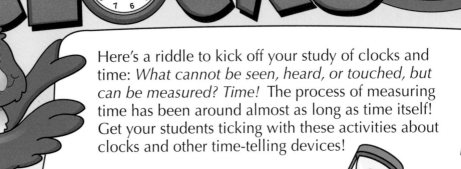

Tick Tock! A time for CLOCKS

Here's a riddle to kick off your study of clocks and time: *What cannot be seen, heard, or touched, but can be measured? Time!* The process of measuring time has been around almost as long as time itself! Get your students ticking with these activities about clocks and other time-telling devices!

DID YOU KNOW?

- One of the first clocks was a stick placed in the center of a circle of 12 rocks. People told the time by where the sun cast a shadow on the rocks.
- Sundials have been used for thousands of years. With sundials, the sun must be shining to tell time!
- Inventors created the first mechanical clocks during the late 1200s.
- The word *clock* comes from the French word *cloche* (klosh) which means *bell*.
- There are many different kinds of clocks besides watches, wall, and digital clocks—sundials, water clocks, hourglasses, chiming clocks, falling dominoes, cuckoo clocks, and more!

LITERATURE SELECTIONS

- ***Clocks and More Clocks*** by Pat Hutchins: Aladdin Paperbacks, 1994. (Picture book, 32 pg.) Mr. Higgins buys more clocks to find one that tells the correct time.
- ***The Time Shop*** by John Kendrick Bangs: Ideal Children's Book, 1998. (Picture book, 40 pg.) A boy gains a new understanding of time.
- ***Telling Time with Big Mama Cat*** by Dan Harper: Harcourt Brace, 1998. (Picture book, 28 pg.) A cat describes her daily routine.

CLOCKS COUNT

Students will be amazed at the number of clocks they find in their own homes. Give each student a Clock Inventory worksheet (page 60). Have students follow the instructions to count the number of clocks in their homes, including analog clocks, digital clocks, and watches. The next day, have students complete a bar graph to show how many analog clocks, how many digital clocks, and how many watches each child has at home.

TIMELY MASTERPIECES

Your students can become horologists (clock makers) and you can teach time-telling skills with these timepieces! To make an analog clock, give each student the following: markers, a 9" paper plate, scissors, and a brad. Have students mark the numbers 1-12 on the plates. Display a real clock for reference. Students can also mark minutes between each of the numbers (four marks between each set of numbers). Copy and cut out one long hand and one short hand pattern (page 60) for each student and use a brad to attach the hands to the clocks.

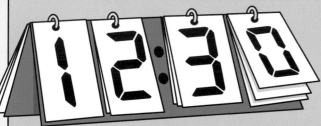

To make a digital clock, give each child copies of the digital numbers 0-9 (page 61), markers, four 4" pieces of string, scissors, and an 8" x 8" piece of poster board. Direct students to fold their pieces of poster board in half to create tent shapes. Make a colon in the center of one side. Make a stack of numbers for each place (see diagram above) and punch a hole near the top of each stack of patterns. Next, thread string through each hole. Punch four holes at the top of each student's poster board tent and loop the string and sets of numbers through the appropriate holes. Have students use both the analog and digital clocks to show specific times.

TAKE FIVE !

Reinforce the concept of telling time and counting by fives. Explain that each of the twelve numbers on a clock is positioned in a five-minute interval. Even though the long hand may be pointing to the *3* on an analog clock, it is not 3 minutes past the hour, but 15 minutes past the hour (*5 + 5 + 5 or 5 x 3 = 15*). Using the paper-plate clocks from *Timely Masterpieces* (above), have students count out loud by fives while manipulating their paper plate clocks to show the correct times.

STOP WATCHIN' THE TIME

Show the class a stopwatch and explain that it is a special type of clock that helps measure specific amounts of time or the amount of time it takes to complete something. Have the class name activities such as *walk to the cafeteria, write 25 spelling words, run one lap around the playground*, etc., and predict the amounts of time it will take to complete these tasks. Allow the class to complete the events and time them using the stopwatch. Write down the actual times and have the class check their predictions. List the activities in order starting with which activity took the least amount of time.

57

THE SCIENCE OF SUNDIALS

Sundials were used long before modern-day clocks were created because people wanted to measure smaller increments of time than just "day" and "night." If possible, bring a real sundial to class. On a sunny day, go outside to observe how shadows are cast on the sundial and other objects. In an hour, return to the sundial and see if the shadows have changed.

Make a class sundial by placing 12 rocks in a circle in an open sunny area. Place a large stick in the ground in the center of the circle of rocks. If possible, do this on the hour, at 1:00, 2:00, etc. Have students identify which rock the stick's shadow is closest to. Adjust the rocks, if necessary, so that the time displayed is as close as possible to the real time. (This may take some trial and error to space the rocks at the right distance apart.) Keep a log of the sundial's time and a clock's time to see how accurate the sundial is versus the regular clock.

TIME-TELLING FRACTIONS

Have a fraction of an hour? Introduce times on the clock which show the fractions quarter and half. Ask if students use the fractional terms *quarter* or *half* when telling time. Cut ¹/₂ and ¹/₄ paper plate sections and place them over the tops of the clocks from *Timely Masterpieces* (page 57). Show students how to position the sections to show that the first 15 minutes equals quarter past the hour and the last 15 minutes equals quarter till the hour. Show them the same thing for half past the hour. Let students use the plate sections as a guide to positioning the clock hands to show quarter past 12, quarter till 12, and half past 12.

ZONIN' OUT

Here's an idea that will take your students around the world! Obtain a map that shows international time zones. Explain that the earth is always spinning, and therefore, the sun's rays are cast onto different parts of the earth throughout the day. Since clock times are based on the sun's position, a clock in one part of the world might read 2:00 pm while a clock in another might read 7:00 pm. Point out the clocks on the time zone map and have the students name the time on each clock, and identify the time zone for your area. Challenge them to name what time it would be in other parts of the world for specific times in your time zone. For example, *If it is 7:00 in the morning here, what time would it be in London, England?* Provide a few manipulative clocks for students to compare different times.

NEW YORK
7:00 am

LONDON
12:00 pm

MOSCOW
3:00 pm

TOKYO
9:00 pm

HONOLULU
2:00 am

MOTHER NATURE'S CLOCK

The Earth is constantly spinning on its axis, even though we cannot feel its movement. The spinning Earth and the sun's rays were the blueprints used by people when early clocks were invented. Place a piece of clay on a globe to mark the location of your hometown. Hold a flashlight above the globe to represent the sun. Slowly turn the globe counterclockwise to simulate the Earth's rotation. Have students observe when the piece of clay is lit by the flashlight's ray. Explain that night and day occur as the sun shines on certain places during certain times of the day. As the globe spins, have students move the hands of a manipulative or real clock as they approximate times of day (depending on the clay's position in relation to the "sun.") Reinforce that the Earth rotates on its axis once in 24 hours; therefore, 24 hours after sunset, sunrise, etc., in your town, it will be the same time of day again. Let students take turns "holding the sun" or "rotating the Earth."

THE GRAINS OF TIME

Students will enjoy using this ancient rice timer! Hourglasses were a popular way to measure time before mechanical clocks were invented. Explain that when an hourglass is turned upside down, sand, rice, or water falls from the top half to the bottom half in a specific amount of time (if it is a true hourglass, then it should take an hour!) When the sand has fallen to the bottom, the hourglass is turned back over to measure the next hour. Gather two matching clean, soda bottles and rice for each timer the class will make. Pour the desired amount of rice into one soda bottle. Place the empty bottle on top of the rice-filled bottle, opening to opening. Use electrical tape to secure the bottles. (The bottles should form an hourglass shape.) Wrap a strip of thin cardboard (as from a cereal box) over the tape, and cover with another layer of tape for support. Predict how long it will take the rice to fall from the top to the bottom. Test the predictions with a clock or stopwatch. Turn the timer over several times for the class to observe that the time it takes for the rice to go from top to the bottom is always the same. Challenge students to create different time measures with different containers.

SPRING FORWARD, FALL BACK

Ask the class if they have heard the saying *Spring Forward, Fall Back*. Discuss how twice a year, in the spring and fall, clocks are adjusted for Daylight Savings Time in most of the United States. Explain that Daylight Savings Time was created (by setting clocks ahead one hour in the spring) so there would be more hours of daylight for activities. In the fall, clocks are set back one hour to standard time, and there are fewer daylight hours. Ask the children if they have noticed that during the summer and spring it gets dark later than in the fall and winter. Have students write descriptive passages about the differences between their spring activities and their fall activities.

59

Clock Inventory

I counted _____ analog clocks.

I counted _____ watches.

I counted _____ digital clocks.

I counted _____ clocks all together.

- -

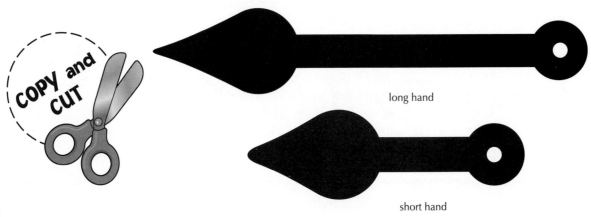

COPY and CUT

long hand

short hand

digital numbers

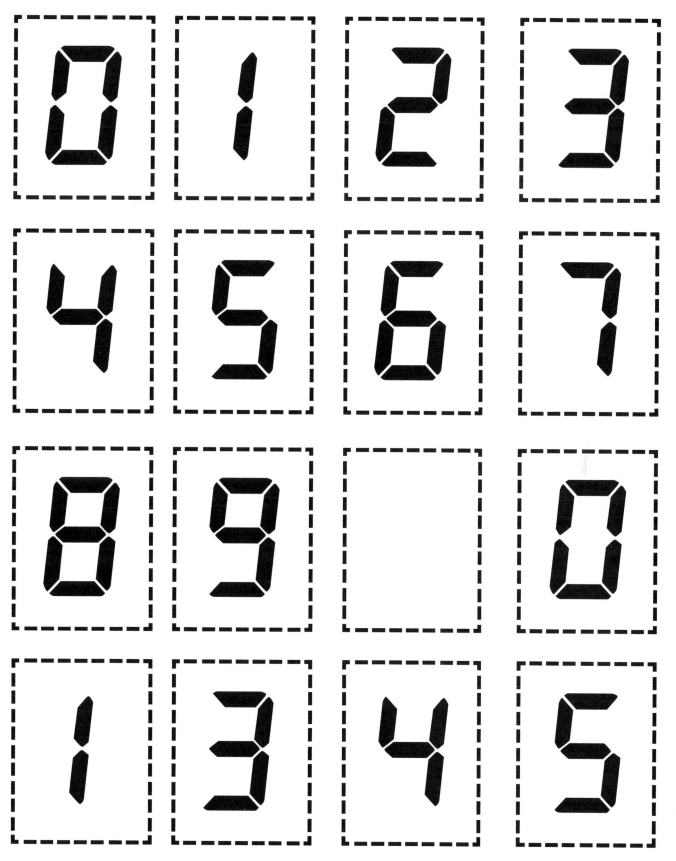

OCTOBER FEAST

Now Serving... PIZZA

Did You Know?

- The first pizzas were made in Italy and had no cheese, only tomatoes and basil leaves!

- The King of Italy asked for a special pizza to honor the queen. The result, Pizza Margherita, represents the colors of the Italian flag with *red* tomatoes, *green* basil leaves, and *white* cheese.

- Pizza came to the United States in 1905 when Gennaro Lombardini moved to New York City and opened the first pizzeria.

Literature Selections

Curious George and the Pizza by Margaret Rey: Houghton Mifflin, 1985 (Picture book, 32 pg.) Curious George gets into trouble in a pizza shop, then helps deliver pizzas.

Hold the Anchovies! A Book About Pizza by Shelley Rotner: Orchard Books, 1996. (Picture book, 32 pg.) Describes the ingredients used to make a pizza.

Pizza Man by Marjorie Pillar: HarperCollins Children's Books, 1990 (Picture book, 40 pg.) Highlights steps to making a pizza.

SING A SONG OF PIZZA

Honor the cheesy pie with this tune!
(Sing to the tune of *Sing a Song of Sixpence*)

Sing a song of pizza,
With mushroom and some cheese!
Lots of yummy toppings and pepperoni, please.
Cut it into slices and take a great big bite.
Pizza! Pizza! Pizza! Pizza!
That's the lunch I like!

Pizza Favorites

Students will think this graphing activity is tops. Have students cut pieces of construction paper into shapes representing their favorite pizza toppings. For example, use red circles for pepperoni, green squares for bell peppers, brown mushroom shapes, etc. Let each student write her name on the shape of her choice. Provide a large tan circle (pizza crust). Have students glue their shapes onto the pizza crust, without overlapping them. Children can count to find out how many people like each topping. Older children can make pizza pie charts using the *Pizza Favorites* results.

Out Of This World Pizza Stories

Create a far-out-pizza-story wheel. Copy and color one pizza pattern (page 70). Cut a paper circle shape the same size. Cut a wedge from the pizza pattern and attach the pizza on top of the circle with a brad. Rotate the circle and write story starters under the pattern. Starters could be: *One day, the pizza maker tossed the pizza so high, it…; The rising pizza dough grew and grew until…;* or *To make a giant pizza, the bakers….* To use the story wheel, turn the pizza pattern until a story starter is visible. Read it aloud and have the class take turns adding to the story. Stories can be recorded and then written out by students. Have students illustrate the stories and bind the pages together into a class book.

To make a giant pizza, the bakers …

Fit for a Queen

Children will love to create pizzas fit for a queen! To make royal pizzas, cut large tan circles from construction paper for students. Let them use tissue paper, yarn, construction paper, etc., to decorate the circles to resemble pizzas. Staple a piece of round writing paper under each pizza, using the pizza as a book cover. On the writing paper, have students write letters to Queen Margherita of Italy telling her why she will love their pizzas. Older students can write jingles or poems praising their creations.

Pizza Pieces

Everyone gets a piece of the pie in this fraction activity! Copy several pizza patterns (page 70). Cut the patterns into halves, thirds, fourths, sixths, and eighths. For older students, cut the patterns into tenths, twelfths, and sixteenths. Give each child a pizza fraction and have him find the other "slices" that belong in his pie. Let the groups put their pies together, then name the fraction that describes how their pizza is divided. Instruct younger students to look for pieces that are the same size. Have older students match different sized pieces to create whole pizzas and name the equivalent fractions. For example, one $\frac{1}{2}$ piece and two $\frac{1}{4}$ pieces make a whole pizza.

Now Serving... Pasta

Did You Know?

- The word *pasta* is an Italian word meaning *paste* or *dough*.
- Flour made from the durum wheat plant is mixed with water to make pasta.
- Some say there are over 600 pasta shapes in Italy.

Literature Selections

Strega Nona by Tomie de Paola: Simon & Schuster Books, 1989. (Picture book, 32 pg.) A modern fable about an Italian Grandmother and her magic pasta-making pot.

Pasta by Kate Haycock: Lerner Publishing, 1990. (Picture book, 32 pg.) Includes information about pasta history and preparation.

Is the Spaghetti Ready? by Frank B. Edwards: Bungalo Books, 1998. (Picture book, 24 pg.) A zookeeper feeds the animals spaghetti!

Let Them Eat Pasta

Have fun by making homemade pasta! Divide the class into small groups. Give each group one egg and one cup of unbleached flour. Follow the instructions below. (Provide plastic gloves for students who will be touching ingredients.)

Pasta

1. Pour the flour on wax paper and make a well, or hollow, in the center. Break the egg into the well.
2. Knead the dough. Add a little water if necessary.
3. Wrap the pasta dough in a clean, damp cloth and place in a refrigerator for 15 minutes.
4. Roll out the dough very thin with a rolling pin. Use plastic knives to cut the dough into long strands or other desired shapes.

When each group has completed the steps, boil the dough shapes for two minutes. (Keep students a safe distance away from boiling water.) If desired, boil a box of dried pasta and heat canned pasta. Allow students to compare the different types of pasta.

Noodley Estimations

How many noodles fit in a jar? During your study of pasta, display three jars of the same size, each containing a different type of pasta. Have students estimate how many pieces of pasta are in each jar. At the end of your study, count the pasta to see whose estimations were closest and which pasta took up the most or least space. Older students can count by 5s, 10s, etc.

Swirl Your Fork around and around...

Let students imagine they have met someone who has never eaten spaghetti! Let the class write stories describing how to eat this delectable pasta dish. Display the delicious stories on a bulletin board.

Shapes of Pasta

Sort out pasta shapes. Bring in different shapes of pasta for students to describe and classify. Pasta can be sorted into tube shapes (macaroni, cannelloni, and penne), twists (fusilli and rotini), long strands (spaghetti, vermicelli), flat strands (linguine, fettuccine), sheets (lasagna), and fun shapes (shells, bowties, wagon wheels, ABCs, etc.). Place various types of pasta in a bowl. Blindfold a student, let her pick out several pieces of pasta, and let her guess which types she selected. For older students, hold a spelling bee using the names of all the pastas.

Pasta Artists

A macaroni mosaic? A rotini rocket? Art pastabilities are endless with dry pasta and creative imaginations! Collect (or have parents donate) a variety of dry pasta shapes. Set up pasta centers with a different variety at each center. Provide scissors, poster board, construction paper, paint, glitter, fabric, foil, yarn, etc., and let students' imaginations run wild!

A Story of Spaghetti

Have a ball of fun with a spaghetti story. Let students sit in a circle. Hold a ball of yellow yarn (to represent spaghetti) and begin a story such as, *The other day, I made a bowl of spaghetti so big that…*. Roll the yarn to a student (holding onto the end) and have him add a sentence to the story. Have him roll the ball to a classmate (while holding onto a section of yarn) who should continue the story. Repeat until each student has added to the story. Tell the last students who receive the yarn to conclude the story. When the story is complete, challenge students to roll the yarn back into a ball without tangling the spaghetti!

Spaghetti Math

Use spaghetti in your classroom in these creative ways!

- Write numbers, number words, and roman numerals with spaghetti.
- Show place value by grouping spaghetti together in tens, hundreds, etc. Then, carefully tie the noodles into bundles with yarn or string.
- Use spaghetti broken in half as tally marks.
- Estimate how many spaghetti noodles it will take to reach across a desk, the classroom, etc., then measure the distance.
- Make shapes such as squares, rectangles, triangles, and pentagons, with spaghetti.

Now serving...
POPCORN

Did You Know?
○ Popcorn is a special kind of corn that has been grown for thousands of years.

○ At the first Thanksgiving in the United States, a Native American brought popcorn to the feast. This began a tradition of giving popcorn as a goodwill offering.

○ Native Americans had popcorn before the arrival of Christopher Columbus. The natives Columbus met in San Salvador wore strings of popcorn in their hair and as necklaces and bracelets.

○ Popcorn, estimated to be 5,600 years old, was discovered by archeologists in Bat Cave, New Mexico.

○ Colonists ate popcorn for breakfast with cream, honey, and fruit!

Literature Selections

The Popcorn Book by Tomie de Paola: Holiday House, 1985. (Picture Book, 32 pg.) Explains the history of popcorn.

The Popcorn Dragon by Jane Thayer: William Morrow and Company, 1989. (Picture book, 32 pg.) A lonely dragon learns that he has special popcorn popping skills.

What Makes Popcorn Pop? by Dave Woodside: Atheneum Publishers, 1980. (Chapter book, 74 pg.) Describes how to grow popcorn and explains what makes it pop.

Popcorn Life Cycle

Where does popcorn come from? Popcorn grows on stalks just like corn on the cob! Talk about how kernels are popped to produce popcorn. Let the children color and cut out copies of the kernel, popcorn, and corn cob patterns (pages 70-71). Provide dental floss and dull-pointed needles. Knot one end of the dental floss and string on several pieces of real popcorn. Use clear tape to attach the patterns in the proper sequence on the dental floss (popcorn at the bottom, kernel in the middle, and corn cob at the top).

Why Does Popcorn POP?

Explain why with this experiment. Popcorn pops because there is water in the center of each kernel. When kernels are heated, steam builds in the pulpy centers of the kernels which explode through the outside shells. Have students pop kernels which have been stored in a refrigerated airtight jar and kernels that have been kept at room temperature. Measure the same amount of kernels, pop them, then count the number of unpopped kernels. Have students determine which storage method produced the most popped kernels. (The kernels kept in the refrigerator will produce the most popped kernels because refrigeration helps kernels keep their moisture.)

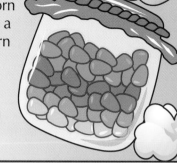

Rainbow Jars

Make rainbow popcorn jars with this art project. Provide colored popcorn kernels. Separate the colors into different containers. Give each child a baby food jar or a clear plastic cup. Have each child choose a popcorn color, fill a small paper cup with the kernels, then pour the kernels into her jar. Allow the students to alternate colors, creating a layered design. When the designs are complete, place the lids on the jars or cover the cups with clear plastic wrap secured with yarn. For a popcorn treat, you can pop the kernels!

Edible Popcorn Jewelry

Native Americans from North America and Mexico used popcorn to made headdresses and jewelry. Aztecs decorated statues with popcorn to honor their gods of Maize, Rain, and Fertility to ensure good crops. Thread a dull-pointed needle through one end of a 24" length of dental floss and knot the opposite end. Provide popcorn, gum drops, and jellybeans, etc., for students to string to make necklaces. Allow students to wear their popcorn necklaces. Students can even eat their necklaces at the end of the day!

Popcorn, Popcorn Everywhere!

A Midwestern U.S. legend describes how the weather was so hot, the popcorn plants in the fields began popping, filling the sky with flying popcorn! People thought it was a blizzard so they dressed warmly and began to shovel the popcorn like snow. Have students write and illustrate stories about popcorn popping in the fields unexpectedly. Let them glue pieces of popped and unpopped popcorn to their pictures.

What's Your Favorite Flavor?

Let your class make fun popcorn flavors! As students make and sample each flavor, have them describe on popcorn patterns (pages 70-71) how it looks, tastes, smells, feels, and sounds. Use the following recipes to flavor three cups of popcorn.

For Cinnamon Sugar Popcorn, shake cinnamon sugar over popcorn.

For Caramel Popcorn, follow the package directions to heat a small jar of caramel sauce. Pour it over the popcorn and mix to evenly coat. Spread the coated popcorn on waxed paper to dry.

For Italian-Flavored Popcorn, melt 1 1/2 tablespoons of butter. Add 1/4 teaspoon each of oregano, parsley, and basil to the butter. Pour the mixture over the popcorn and toss to coat.

For Orange Popcorn, place popcorn in a bowl and spray with cooking spray. Sprinkle 3 tablespoons of orange drink mix and 1/2 teaspoon dried orange peel. Toss the popcorn to coat evenly.

Now serving... *Desserts*

Did You Know?

❀ The world's largest Boston cream pie, baked to celebrate the 350th birthday of Boston, weighed 3,800 pounds! The world's largest chocolate chip cookie weighed 474 pounds!

❀ Two popular dessert traditions include making a wish and blowing out candles on birthday cakes and serving cake at weddings. At many weddings, the bride and groom feed each other cake before the guests are served.

Literature Selections

❀ ***The Magic School Bus Gets Baked in a Cake: A Book about Kitchen Chemistry*** by Joanna Cole: Scholastic, 1995. (Picture book, 32 pg.) The class tries to bake a cake, but ends up inside it!

❀ ***Electra and the Charlette Russe*** by Corinne Demas Bliss: Boyds Mills, 1997. (Picture book, 32 pg.) Electra tries to repair the damage on special pastry desserts.

Bakery Business

Take a sweet field trip to a local bakery (many grocery stores have their own bakeries) and let students see what goes into preparing and decorating pastries, cakes, and other delectable treats.

Thanks for the Taste, Bud

Desserts are beautiful to see and delightful to smell, but what most of us enjoy is their tastes! Ask students if they would enjoy eating desserts if they could not taste them. Explain that our tongues and the roofs of our mouths are covered with thousands of tiny taste buds. Cells in our taste buds send messages to the brain and the brain tells us what flavor we are eating. Taste buds recognize four basic tastes: sweet, salty, sour, and bitter. Ask students which taste is their favorite and which they think most desserts are. Explain that because most desserts contain sugar, most are considered sweet. Before the lesson, make two batches of cookies. Make the first batch according to the recipe. With the second batch, change the recipe so that the sweet ingredients (such as sugar or chocolate chips) are left out or are unsweetened. Give each student a cookie from each batch and see if she can guess which is sweet and which is not-so-sweet!

Batter Matter

Explain that cooking chemistry happens when ingredients are mixed together and then heated or cooled. Have students bring in the necessary ingredients for making a cake. Have them name each ingredient and then mix them together. Tell students that the combined ingredients form a new chemical substance, the batter for the cake. Ask if the batter is a liquid, solid, or gas (it is a liquid). Ask what they think would happen if the batter was placed into a freezer (the batter would become thicker, possibly freezing into a solid). Pour the batter into a baking dish and bake according to the recipe. (Be sure to keep students a safe distance away from the oven.) When the cake has baked, ask students to identify the steam rising from the cake (gas). After the cake has cooled, allow the class to enjoy the solid—the cake itself!

 ## Cooperative Pumpkin Pies

Make pumpkin pies to celebrate both October and Dessert Month. Divide the class into 2-4 cooking groups. Give each group a mixing bowl, a large spoon, one 8" pie shell, and the eggs, pumpkin, and evaporated milk as listed below. Set up a measuring center with a measuring cup, measuring spoons, bowls of granulated sugar, salt, ground cinnamon, ginger, and cloves. List the ingredient amounts on the board and direct each group to work together to make the pie filling.

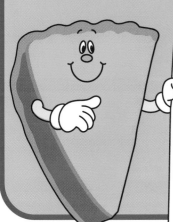

Mix the ingredients below in the order listed, and add to the pie shell:

2 eggs lightly beaten
one 16-ounce can solid pack pumpkin
3/4 cup sugar
1/2 teaspoon salt
1 teaspoon ground cinnamon
1/2 teaspoon ground ginger
1/4 teaspoon ground cloves
one 12-ounce can of evaporated milk

After the ingredients are mixed, have each group spoon the mixture into a pie shell. Preheat an oven to 425° with two baking sheets inside. Place the pies on the baking sheets and bake for 15 minutes. Reduce the temperature to 350° and bake for 20-30 minutes (if a toothpick inserted into the filling comes out clean, the pie is ready!). Enjoy the pumpkin treat with whipped cream on top!

  ## Sweetie Pizza Pie

Pizza for dessert? Definitely! To make this fruity, nutritious pie, provide refrigerated sugar cookie dough, whipped topping or cream cheese, and fruit, such as pineapple, strawberries, and kiwi, sliced into small pieces. Press the cookie dough onto a round baking sheet and bake according to the package directions. After the cookie has cooled, spread whipped topping over the cookie. Then, top with fruit. What a sweetie pie!

69

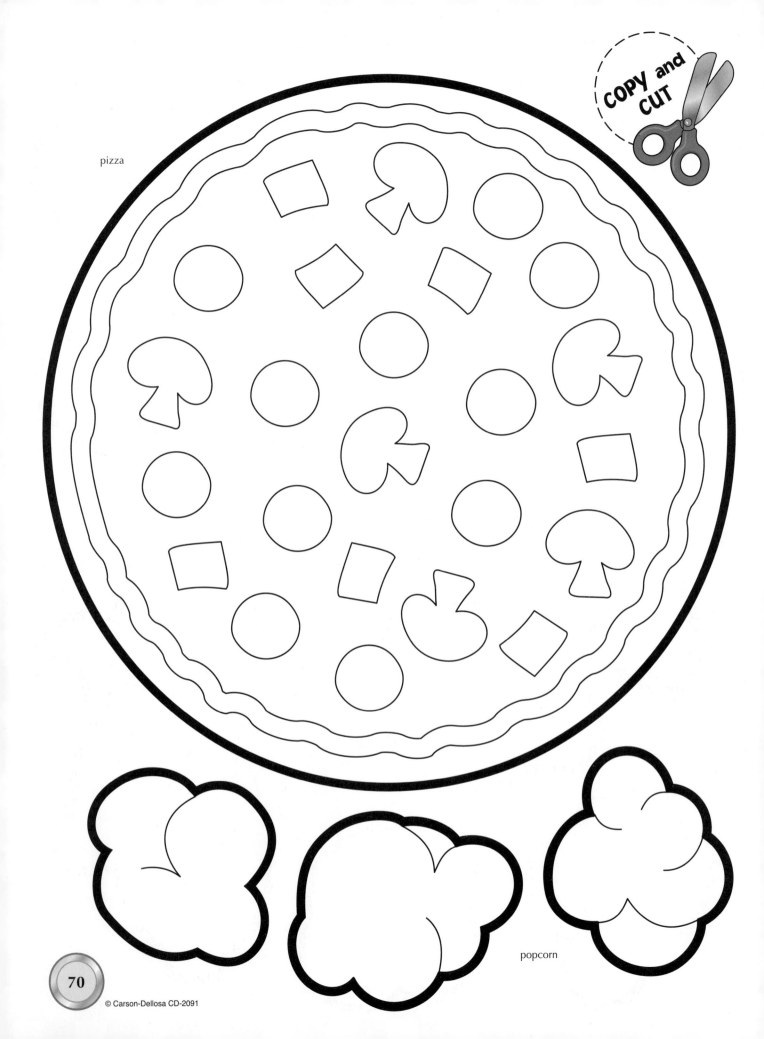

pizza

COPY and CUT

popcorn

70

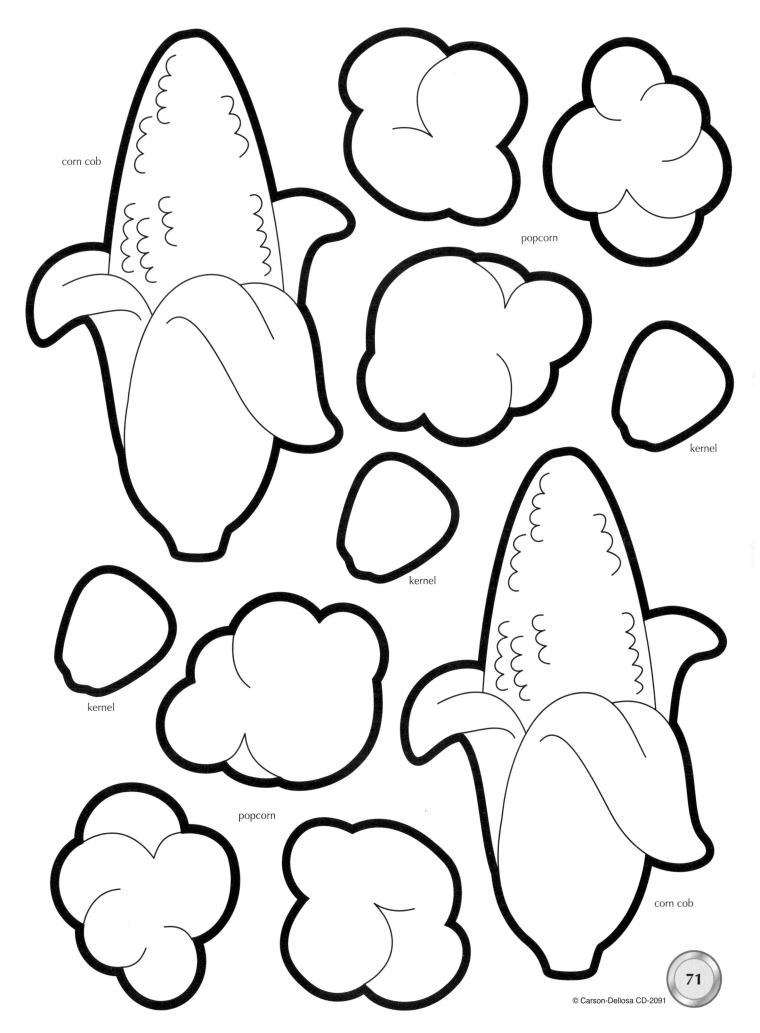

corn cob

popcorn

kernel

kernel

kernel

popcorn

corn cob

71

Look It Up!
Dictionary Day

Ever want to tell your students to "Look it up?" Use these interactive activities to teach important dictionary skills.

Did You Know?

• Noah Webster was a lexicographer, which means he wrote dictionaries. His birthday, October 16, 1758, is also known as Dictionary Day. In 1828, after 20 years of work, Webster published the first American dictionary, *An American Dictionary of the English Language*. Webster was also a teacher, writer, newspaper editor, and helped found Amherst College in Amherst, Massachusettes.

• Early dictionaries only listed very difficult words.

• The first comprehensive English dictionary was made in England in 1755 by Samuel Johnson.

Anita   Bobby   Corey   David   Eileen   Freddie

GO ALPHABETICAL!

Alphabetize your class with this fun activity! Show guide words at the tops of dictionary pages. Explain that the first guide word tells what entry appears first on the page and the last guide word tells what entry appears last. Have each student write her name in large print on construction paper. Choose two students to come to the front of the room with their names to be guide words. Students whose names would appear on a dictionary page with those guide words should come to the front of the room and alphabetize themselves between the two guide-word students. Repeat the activity several times with different guide-word names and then challenge the entire class to line up alphabetically. Continue the lesson through the day by lining up alphabetically for lunch, assemblies, etc.

Ready, Set, Look It Up!

Check students' speed and accuracy with a dictionary race. Divide the class into two teams and place two dictionaries on a table. Have a student from each team come to the table. Call out a word and say "Look It Up!" The first student to find the word in his dictionary wins a point for his team. For an added challenge, give students the pronunciation of a word (for example, **a**-pəl: apple), and have them race to look up the word.

A Picture Is Worth a Thousand Words

Picture students as lexicographers as they create their own picture dictionaries. In a picture dictionary, all entries have a picture and sometimes a short definition to accompany it. Write fall words on the board, such as acorn, pumpkin, etc. Have students write the words in large letters in the top right corners of horizontal half-sheets of paper. Then, ask them to draw a picture of each word. Let each student create a cover and compile his pages into personal fall picture dictionaries. Donate the completed picture dictionaries to younger students, if desired.

Where's My Definition?

Use this interactive activity to teach words and their definitions. Write simple words on index cards and definitions on separate index cards. Give each student a card and tell them to walk quietly around the classroom, trying to find their partner. Once the "word" and "definition" find each other, have them write a sentence together that uses their word correctly. Share the words, definitions, and sentences with the class.

Parts of Speech Sentences

Help students find the part of speech identifier. Open a dictionary at random and find two nouns and a verb. Then, challenge students to write a sentence using those words, as well as adjectives, and/or adverbs in their sentences. Share the sentences with the class.

Mixed Up Cooperation

Learn the parts of a definition with this cooperative exercise. Make two sets of the different components of a dictionary entry on sentence strips. For example, write the word on one strip, pronunciation on another, etc. Place the sets of strips at two tables. Choose two teams of two students to come to the front of the room. Say "Go!" and have each group place the cards in order as they would appear in a dictionary entry. To make the activity more challenging for older students, mix several words and their components together to sort and match.

round, orange fruit that grows on the ground

73

Scrambled Syl-la-bles

Break up a word and put it back together with this syllable activity. Entry words are broken into syllables to help with pronunciation. Show how syllables are broken up in the dictionary, then clap or tap out syllables of several familiar words. Display a list of spelling and vocabulary words, and ask students to pick 6-7 words to break into syllables and then check in the dictionary. Then, have students scramble the syllables and write the scrambled syllables on another sheet of paper. For the word *com-put-er*, for example, a student may write *put-com-er*. After the syllables are scrambled, let students exchange papers and try to figure out each other's scrambled words.

Coin a Phrase

Pizzarama? Comp Time? Coin new words or phrases and make dictionary pages representing them. Students can also define slang words they use in school and at home. Be sure to include the word, definition, part of speech, and a sample sentence for each new word they coin. Illustrate the words, if appropriate.

Diccionario De La Lenguaje

What's the Spanish word? Explain that there are several types of dictionaries. For English speakers, foreign language dictionaries have two sections, one with an English word entry and foreign word equivalent, and the other with a foreign word entry and the English definition. Assign each student a simple word, such as a color or number word, names of classroom items, etc., and give them the translation in one foreign language of your choice. Have students write the words and translations on index cards and label classroom items with the correct words. Then, make two dictionary pages, one with an English entry and the other with a foreign language entry. Illustrate the entries, if applicable. Bind the finished pages into a dictionary with the English entries in the front and the foreign language entries in the back.

PUMPKIN PATCH FUN

October is the time of year for dressing in costumes, carving jack-o'-lanterns, and displaying creepy skeletons and spiders! Put a twist on your traditional celebrations with these innovative ideas for teaching exciting October subjects!

PUMPKINS AND JACK-O'-LANTERNS

Did You Know?

- Pumpkins are a variety of squash and are vegetables, not fruits. Like other squash, they grow on the ground on vines.
- Pumpkins start out green, then gradually change to orange as they grow bigger.
- Native Americans grew pumpkins and taught early settlers how to grow them.
- Originally, jack-o'-lanterns were made by placing candles inside hollowed out turnips, beets, or potatoes! After settling in the U.S., immigrants found pumpkins were better for making jack-o'-lanterns.

Literature Selections

Pumpkin Pumpkin by Jeanne Titherington: Mulberry Books, 1990. (Picture book, 23 pg.) A boy grows a large pumpkin from a seed, carves it, and saves seeds to plant the next year.

Five Little Pumpkins by Iris Van Rynbach: Boyds Mills Press, 1995. (Picture book, 24 pg.) Illustrated version of the popular finger play rhyme.

Too Many Pumpkins by Linda White: Holiday House, 1997. (Picture book, 32 pg.) A woman who hates pumpkins makes the best of it when pumpkins sprout in her yard.

Funny Jack-o'-Lantern

Sing to the tune of *Twinkle, Twinkle Little Star*
Pumpkin, pumpkin orange and round
(Students make arms into a big circle)
Pumpkin, pumpkin on the ground
(Students squat to the ground)
Farmer, farmer look at me
(Students point to self)
What a funny jack-o'-lantern I would be
(Students jump up and spread arms wide and smile or make a face)
Pumpkin, pumpkin orange and round
(Students make arms into a big circle)
Pumpkin, pumpkin on the ground
(Students squat to the ground)

Carved in Pumpkin

Make shapely pumpkin names with your class. Have each child draw the outline of a large pumpkin on orange construction paper. Inside the pumpkin, have each student draw connecting bubble letters of her name, filling the space inside the pumpkin. Next, carefully cut out the letters, without cutting them apart. Finally, cut a green paper stem and leaf and glue them to the pumpkin name. Display the pumpkin names around the classroom.

How Does a Pumpkin Grow?

Pick some pumpkin facts and learn about a pumpkin's life cycle. Explain that pumpkins grow from seeds. When the seeds sprout leaves, the pumpkin vines begin to grow. Soon, small yellow flowers bloom on the vines. Small green bulbs, which are actually tiny pumpkins, develop under the flowers. As the tiny green pumpkins grow larger, they begin to turn orange. Using the seed, flower, and small pumpkin patterns (page 84), have students illustrate the pumpkin life cycle. Give each child a green pipe cleaner. Have him tape each pattern in the correct sequence on the pipe cleaner. Mount the completed pipe cleaners on construction paper along with a few sentences describing a pumpkin's life cycle.

The Life of a Pumpkin
Pumpkins grow from small seeds. The seeds sprout, and a vine begins to grow. Then small yellow flowers bloom on the vine. Below the flowers, a green bulb grows. The green bulb soon begins to change colors. Once it is completely orange, the pumpkin is ready to be picked!

Jack-o'-Lantern Storytelling

Creative stories will write themselves with this cooperative activity. Write seasonal nouns and sound words on pumpkin patterns (page 84). Possible words include *jack-o'-lantern, pumpkin, costume, mask, scarecrow, spider, leaf, Boom!, Squeek!,* and *Poof!* Label several patterns with *The End*. Place the patterns in a plastic pumpkin. Have each child choose a pattern and begin a story with a sentence or two using the word on the pattern. Then, she should pass the pattern to a classmate. Have the second child choose a word and add to the story, incorporating his new word. If a student chooses a card that says *The End*, he must compose an ending to the story.

ONCE UPON A TIME. . . THERE WAS A HANDSOME PUMPKIN NAMED JACK. JACK LIVED IN A MAGIC PUMPKIN PATCH UNDER THE SHADOW. . . OF THE MOON. ONE NIGHT, JACK DECIDED TO WALK TO . . .

My Pumpkin
My pumpkin has a large smile. His nose is a circle and his eyes are shaped like gumdrops.

Do You See What I See?

Follow directions to make a jack-o'-lantern. Have each child draw a jack-o'-lantern face on a pumpkin pattern (page 84) and write several sentences describing the face he has drawn. Have the children pass their descriptions, along with blank pumpkin patterns to a partner. Instruct the partner to draw a jack-o'-lantern face using only the written description. Compare the new drawing to the original. Talk about the importance of including details and complete information when writing. Next, have students rewrite their descriptions with more detail and complete the activity with a different partner.

Tell Me About Your Pumpkin

Learn all about pumpkins with this math-centered activity. Provide pumpkins of various shapes and sizes for students to measure. Let students make general observatios about the pumpkins, such as tall, round, etc. Then, divide the class into small groups and give each group a pumpkin and a pumpkin pattern (page 84) to record their findings. First, to measure the circumference, wrap a string around the fattest part, then measure the length of the string. Second, to measure diameter, place one side of the pumpkin against a wall, then place a flat object, such as a book, against the opposite side. Measure the distance between the two flat surfaces to find the diameter of the pumpkin. Third, to measure height, place a flat object on top of the pumpkin, and measure the distance from the flat object to the floor. Last, have students weigh the pumpkins on a bathroom scale. Display the completed patterns and have students compare their results. Emphasize that pumpkins, like humans, come in different shapes and sizes, and each is special in its own way!

Mirror Images

Mirror images will appear with this exercise in symmetry. Provide orange and black 11" x 17" construction paper for each student. Have students cut the black piece in half, then cut one side curved like the side of a pumpkin. Tell students to glue the black scrap piece on the right edge of the orange construction paper (see diagram). From the black pumpkin half, have children cut out one eye, half nose, and half mouth. Have students glue the completed black pumpkin half on the right side of the orange paper, matching the straight edge to the middle of the paper. Have children glue the black cut out facial features to the orange side, matching them up accordingly.

Seed What's Inside

How many seeds are in a pumpkin? Find out by counting them! Provide a pumpkin and have students estimate how many seeds are in it. Enlarge one pumpkin pattern (page 84) and write each child's guess with her name on the pattern. Cover a work area with newspaper. Cut the top off the pumpkin and give each student a scoop of pulp. Have them separate the seeds and count them. Then, add each child's number to get a class total and compare with the estimates. If desired, let children design the face to be carved. After the activity, you can roast and salt the seeds for a tasty snack.

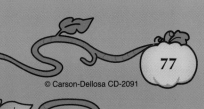

77

DRESS UP!

Did You Know?

- Dressing up in costumes for All Hallows Day (the day after Halloween) started in the Middle Ages.
- Kings and queens, like King Henry VIII of England and King Louis XV of France, often gave costume parties.
- Wearing masks is common in ceremonies around the world. Even prehistoric cave dwellers wore masks!

Literature Selections

The Magic Costumes by Jamie Lehrer: Dial Books for Young Readers, 1996. (Pop-Up book, 24 pg.) Children find a magic costume box.
Costumes and Clothes by Jean Cooke: The Bookwright Press, 1987. (Non-fiction book, 32 pg.) Describes international dress throughout the ages.

Around the World in Your Class

People around the world wear different types of clothing for different reasons. Break students into groups and assign each group a country or region. Help students research traditional dress in the country, and list when costumes are worn, what they are made from, who wears them, etc. Provide art materials such as bulletin board paper, fabric scraps, paints, beads, glitter, etc., and challenge each group to create a child-size costume which showcases the traditional dress of the country they researched. Then, have each group present their costume and country information to the class. Display the completed costumes on classroom walls for a trip around the world!

Masquerade Ball

Invite students to masquerade as someone else! Copy a mask pattern (page 85) on oaktag for each student. Measure a length of elastic and tie at the holes indicated on the pattern or tape one edge to a craft stick. Provide a variety of craft materials such as feathers, sequins, construction paper, etc., and let each student design a mask for himself. When all of the masks are finished and the glue has dried, have a masquerade party with dancing and snacks!

Career Costumes

Every career has a different costume. Talk about careers and the uniforms that workers wear. Provide props and dress-up clothes such as hats, play tools, coats, work shirts, etc. Allow groups of students to dress up in the career clothes of their choice and have their photos taken. Then, make a strand of paper dolls, with one doll for each student. Let each student decorate one doll in the clothing or uniform that he chose. Display the completed paper doll chain along with the photos on a classroom wall.

BONING UP
on the Human Skeleton

Did You Know?

- Babies have over 300 bones at birth that gradually fuse together to form the 206 bones of an adult. Babies' bones are made mostly of cartilage that hardens, or calcifies, as they grow.

- Calcium in milk products helps bones grow, but spinach and broccoli are good sources of calcium, too!
- People shrink during the day! Liquid in cartilage disks between vertebrae leaks out from the pressure of standing and is replaced while we sleep.
- The jawbone is the hardest bone in the body.
- Nearly half of your bones are in your hands and feet.

Literature Selections

Bones: Our Skeletal System by Seymour Simon: Morrow Junior, 1998. (Non-fiction book, 32 pg.) Describes the skeletal system and outlines the important roles bones play in the human body.
Boogie Bones by Elizabeth Loredo: Putnam Publishing Group, 1997. (Picture book, 32 pg.) Boogie Bones is a skeleton who enters a dance contest.
Dem Bones by Bob Barner: Chronicle Books, 1996. (Picture book, 32 pg.) Classic African-American story also includes factual information about bones. .

Cooperation Skeleton Display

Have students work together to learn about their bones as they construct a skeleton. Place bulletin board paper vertically on the floor. Let each student add a bone to the skeleton, and tell its name and function. The following materials are needed for the skeleton construction: 1 skull—paper plate, 26 vertebrae—white rings of paper, 24 total ribs—short cardboard tubes, 2 collar bones—long cardboard tubes, 12 arm and leg bones—8 long cardboard tubes with 4 long straws for ulnas and fibulas, 2 hip bones—paper plates, 20 hand and foot bones—regular drinking straws cut into thirds, 56 total finger and toe bones—stirring straws cut into sections (3 on each finger and toe and 2 on thumbs and big toes).

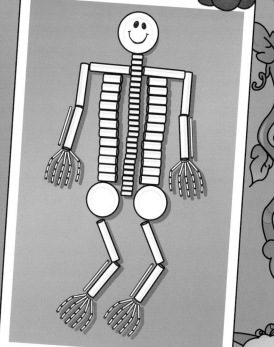

How is an Elbow Like a Door?

Find out! Break students into groups and give each a door hinge (or have them examine the hinges on a door) and two short cardboard tubes with a ping-pong ball between them. Let students experiment with the movement of the hinge and the cardboard tubes and challenge them to figure out which of their joints acts like which model. Explain that the ping-pong ball and cardboard tubes model shows a ball and socket joint like your shoulders and hips, and the hinge shows a hinge joint like your knees and elbows.

Get Dressed for a Trip

Many invertebrate animals, like jellyfish, do not have bones! Humans are vertebrates because we have skeletons that give us our shape and support our muscles, organs, and skin. Ask students to stand up and act like jellyfish. Then, show students a shirt on a hanger and explain that the hanger gives the shirt its shape. If you take the shirt off the hanger, its shape is gone. In addition to bone, a flexible material called cartilage also gives parts of our bodies shape. Let students feel the tops of their ears and the tips of their noses for cartilage. Next, have students feel their bones through their skin (fingers, wrists, shins, ankles, backbones, ribs, etc.). Challenge each student to draw a bone with white chalk on black construction paper, by guessing what it looks like based on how it feels.

Protective Gear

Show students how bones protect delicate organs from injury with peek-inside books. The skull is a protective shell for the brain; the ribs form a cage for the heart and lungs; the backbone surrounds the sensitive spinal cord, and the pelvic bone protects lower abdominal organs, such as intestines and bladder. To make a peek-inside book, have each student fold a piece of construction paper and then fold the two sides to meet in the middle. Glue the outside skeleton pattern (page 86) to the outside of the paper and then cut as indicted on the pattern to divide the skeleton in half vertically, and then horizontally into four sections. On the inside, glue the inside skeleton pattern (page 86) to the page. Now, when students open their peek-inside books, they will be able to see which body parts are protecting which organs.

How Do Your Bones Measure Up?

The longest bone in your body is the femur, or thigh bone, and the shortest bone is the stirrup bone in the ear! Let students measure bones, such as fingers, forearms, etc., and the circumference of their skulls. Each student can add her head, back, and leg measurements together to estimate her height, then measure her actual height with a yard stick. Challenge older students to figure out how to tell if their femur is really equal to $1/4$ of their total height, as it is claimed to be.

Look Inside

Build a bone from the inside out! Ask students to describe what they think a bone looks like on the inside. Then, explain (showing with a soup bone, if possible) that bones have holes in them which make them light and strong. Bones also contain marrow, a soft substance that makes new blood for the body. To make a model of a bone's inside, gather long cardboard tubes cut into 3" lengths, pink household sponges split to half thickness, and play dough. Divide students into small groups. Each group should roll up a section of sponge and stuff it inside the cardboard tube, then fill the center opening with play dough. Explain to the students how the model reflects the inside of a real bone.

Posable Skeleton

This posable skeleton will tickle students' funny bones! Give each student six white pipe cleaners. Use one pipe cleaner as a spine. Attach one pipe cleaner to the bottom of the spine, bending it down to form legs, and one on top, bending it up to form arms. Twist the ends of two pipe cleaners together and attach to the spine, under the arms. Loop it around front and wrap it around the spine. Repeat several times to make a rib cage. Attach the last pipe cleaner to the top and coil to make a skull. Allow students to bend and pose their skeletons.

Take Your Skeleton for a Dip

Make a calcium rich skeleton snack! Chop up veggies and arrange them on a platter to look like a skeleton. Use cucumber slices as vertebrae, broccoli, bell pepper slices, celery, and carrot sticks for arms, legs, and ribs. In a bowl, mix sour cream with dry onion soup mix and place at the top, as the head. Dip in and enjoy!

81

SPECTACULAR SPIDERS

Did You Know?
- Spiders first lived about 300 million years ago, before dinosaurs existed!
- Spiders have eight legs and most have eight eyes (two large eyes and six small eyes).
- All spiders can produce silk, but not all spiders spin webs.
- Although spiders have venom, very few spiders are harmful to humans.
- Spiders are shy and avoid people whenever possible.
- Spiders eat many insects that can damage crops.

Literature Selections
Dream Weaver by Jonathan London: Harcourt Brace, 1998. (Picture book, 32 pg.) A boy imagines he is a spider.
Outside and Inside Spiders by Sandra Markle: Atheneum, 1994. (Non-fiction book, 40 pg.) Describes habitat, lifestyle, and mating of spiders.
The Lady and the Spider by Faith McNulty: HarperCollins, 1987. (Picture book, 48 pg.) A spider who lives in a head of lettuce is put back into the garden.

A Spider's Life

Spin the tale of a spider's life cycle with this craft. Have students illustrate a spider's life cycle using a large construction paper circle divided into 4 equal sections.

Section 1: Have students draw a twig and a leaf and glue a small cotton ball to the twig to resemble a silk egg sac.

Section 2: Show spiderlings (baby spiders!) hatching by repeating the twig and leaf and drawing tiny spiders on them.

Section 3: Draw several spiderlings with small pieces of thread glued to each to show ballooning (when spiderlings spin long strands of silk, which are caught by breezes and carry them away).

Section 4: Show molting, or shedding of outer skin, by drawing one spider and cutting a duplicate of the spider from tissue paper. Glue the tissue paper spider beside the drawn spider to represent its shed exoskeleton.

When the craft is complete, have students write short descriptions of each step of the life cycle on the backs of the appropriate sections.

I'm Misunderstood! Students are the spiders in this activity. Read the *Did You Know?* facts (above) and discuss how spiders are helpful to people. Cut a 12" circle from writing paper for each student. Have each student write a letter on his paper from the point of view of a spider. Glue the completed letters to black construction paper circles which are slightly larger than the writing papers. Then, glue a smaller black construction paper circle to the large circle for the spider's head. Add 2 (or 2 large and 6 small) wiggly eyes and bent black pipe cleaners on each side for the spider's legs.

Spiders Vs. Insects

Explain that spiders are arachnids, not insects. Share facts about spiders and insects with students to help them determine their differences. Have students create comparison charts by folding construction paper in half to create columns. Students should label the columns *Spiders* and *Insects* and write facts in the appropriate columns. Next, using washable inkpads, have each student make a spider and an insect above the correct column . To make a spider, make a thumbprint, then a print of the pinky finger for the spider's head. Then, draw eight legs and two mouth parts, or *pedipalps*. To make an insect, make three fingerprints in a row using the index finger. Then, draw six legs, two antennae, and two wings. Provide nature magazines and allow students to cut out pictures of insects and spiders to place in the appropriate columns.

INSECTS	SPIDERS
• Have 3 body parts	• Have 2 body parts
• Have 6 legs	• Have 8 legs
• Have 2 antenna on their heads	• Have 2 mouth parts called pedipalps
• May have wings	• Do not have wings

What's for Dinner?

Because spiders have no teeth, they must turn their food into liquid so they can eat it! To eat, spiders use fangs to inject venom into insects. This venom turns the insides of the prey into a liquid. Then, spiders use their pedipalps to squeeze the fluids from the bodies of the prey. To demonstrate this, give each child a sugar cube. Let them feel how hard the cube is, similar to an insect. Have students use eyedroppers to add several drops of warm water to the cube and compare the dissolving sugar cube to the breaking down of the insides of insects. Then, talk about how spiders have special abilities that allow them to compensate for their lack of teeth.

Hungry Spiders!

Spiders that do not spin webs use other methods to catch insects. Find out how with this craft illustrating how spiders hunt. Divide a piece of construction paper into three sections. Label the sections *Jumping, Camouflage,* and *Trapdoor.*

Jumping spiders hide and wait for their prey, then pounce on it. For the jumping spider, cut a small circle and four strips from black construction paper. Tape or glue the strips under the circle for legs. Then, accordion fold a small strip of paper. Attach one end to the spider and the other end to the paper. Draw leaves and rocks around the spider as hiding places.

Camouflage spiders are the same color as the flowers or plants they hide inside. When an insect lands, the spider attacks it. For the camouflage spider, draw a flower and cut out a spider that is the same color and glue it inside the flower.

Trapdoor spiders dig burrows about 6-8" underground, complete with a tight-fitting trapdoor attached to the ground on one side with silk and covered with leaves and dirt. When an insect approaches the trapdoor, the spider pops out and pulls it inside. For the trapdoor spider, cut out a small circle and tape it down on the top only. Draw leaves and grass over the trapdoor, then lift the door and draw a spider under it.

83

pumpkin
(also use with bulletin board idea pg. 17)

seed

flower

small pumpkin

84

© Carson-Dellosa CD-2091

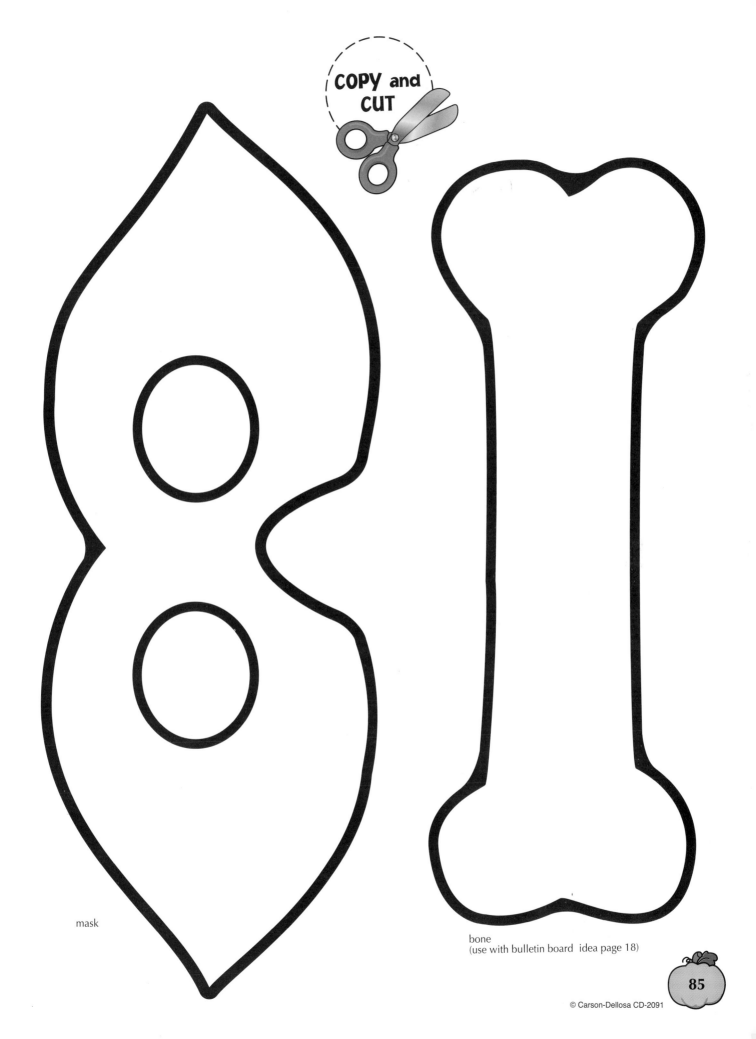

COPY and CUT

mask

bone
(use with bulletin board idea page 18)

85

© Carson-Dellosa CD-2091

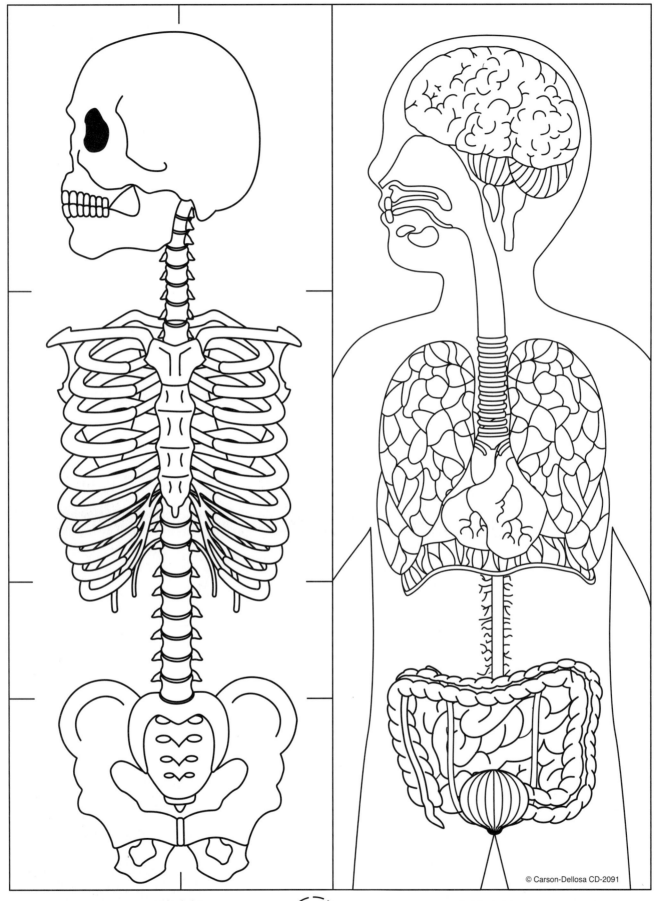

outside skeleton   inside skeleton

COPY and CUT

Our NOCTURNAL NEIGHBORS

Nocturnal animals are bewitching and enchanting, a little spooky, and oh, so mysterious. They are fascinating creatures who are often the subject of misunderstanding, superstition, and fear because of their nighttime ways. Explore nature's nighttime wonders with these pages of activities about owls, raccoons, opossums, and bats!

Did You Know?

🌙 The word *nocturnal* means *active at night*. When an animal is classified as nocturnal, it means that the animal sleeps during the day and is awake at night.

🌙 There are hundreds of nocturnal animals and insects, including raccoons, bats, opossums, owls, mice, cockroaches, porcupines, wolves, skunks, and fireflies.

🌙 Nocturnal animals have strong senses which enable them to see in the dark and hear noises far away.

LITERATURE SELECTIONS

Night Creatures
by Sylvaine Perols: Scholastic Trade, 1998. (Picture book, 24 pg.) An introduction to night animals, focusing on owls and bats.

The Goodnight Circle
by Carolyn Lesser: Harcourt Brace, 1984. (Picture book, 32 pg.) Describes the activities of animals from dusk till dawn.

Life in the Dark
by Joyce Pope: Raintree Steck-Vaughn, 1992. (Picture book, 48 pg.) Describes the habitat and activities of night animals.

Nighttime Senses

Show students the sharp senses of nighttime creatures. Discuss how nocturnal animals have senses like humans, but some senses are more acute, allowing them to survive at night. Have students name the five senses and how they think the senses of sight and smell help night animals hunt for food and travel in the dark. Turn off the lights and have students cover their eyes to simulate nighttime. Then, have them listen for sounds you make by tapping classroom objects or using a sound-effects tape. Challenge students to name the sounds using only their sense of hearing. Next, have students stand on one side of the classroom while you stand on the other. Turn off the lights to make the classroom as dark as possible. Hold up objects to see if students can identify them using their "night vision." Explain that most nocturnal animals see in the night as well as most humans see in the day.

Nocturnal Crayon Resist

With this nifty nighttime craft you can teach whooo's out at night. Have on hand several resources showing nocturnal animals. Let students use crayons on white construction paper to illustrate an outdoor scene showing several different night animals. Tell students to use dark, heavy strokes with the crayons. After the students have finished their illustrations, have them use black watercolor paint, diluted with water, to paint over the pictures. The paint will resist the crayon strokes to give the illusion of the night.

87

Go BATTY About BATS!

When the Sun Goes Down
(Sing to the tune of
Row, Row, Row Your Boat)

When the sun goes down
Bats will come outside
Through the dark
They fly around
With echoes as their guides.

Did You Know?

- Bats are the only mammals that can fly.
- *Blind as a bat* is not accurate because many types of bats have extremely good vision.
- There are nearly one thousand varieties of bats. The largest has a wing span of almost 6' and the smallest weighs less than a penny!
- Bats sleep hanging upside down from their feet. This is called *roosting*.
- Some people, especially in China and Japan, regard the bat as a sign of good luck, happiness, and long life.

Echoes in the Night

While most bats have excellent eyesight, their sense of hearing aids them most when navigating and hunting for food at night. Explain echolocation to the students. Echolocation works with a bat's high-pitched sound (inaudible to human ears) made while flying. This sound bounces off objects and sends an echo back to the bat. The echo helps the bat determine if there is an insect close by, food, or an object in its path that it must navigate around. Show pictures of bats to the students so they can observe how bats' ears are bowl-shaped to enable them to "catch" sounds better. Play this fun echolocation game and have students use sounds to find each other. Take the class to an open area and choose a student to be the bat. Blindfold the "bat" or have him close his eyes. Once the bat is blindfolded and ready to begin, have the other students decide if they want to be obstacles or insects. Tell students who are obstacles to find a place to sit, stand, or lie down. They are not to move. Students who are insects should slowly move around the obstacles. Tell the bat to walk around the area and emit a high-pitched *Beep!* each time he wants to know what lies in his path. Any child in the bat's path must respond with the appropriate sound (such as *Bam!* for obstacles or *Yikes!* for insects), depending on what part the child is playing. The bat should attempt to tag insects and avoid obstacles. The first tagged insect becomes the next bat. The bat becomes an obstacle, and obstacles become insects. Rotating roles will allow the students to learn about the entire echolocation process.

Bat Tangram

Help students practice problem-solving skills while creating adorable tangram bats. Give each student a copy of the tangram pattern *(page 54)*. Have students carefully cut out the patterns and glue them to construction paper to create a bat shape. See the illustrations for reference of the completed bat. (If you have younger students, you may want to complete a bat tangram and display it for reference.) If desired, provide wiggly eyes for students to glue onto their bats.

PLAYIN' POSSUM

Did You Know?

- Opossums are the only North American marsupials, which means females have pouches for their young, like kangaroos.

- Opossums have been called "nature's sanitation engineers" because they help maintain a clean, healthy environment by eating insects and rodents.

- Opossums are often depicted in illustrations hanging upside down from tree limbs. Adult opossums are actually too heavy to do this, but occasionally a baby possum may hang upside down for a short time.

- Opossums have inhabited the earth since the time of the dinosaur!

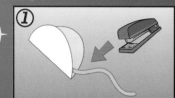

Get Crafty with Opossums

Nighttime creativity will come out in this opossum craft. 1. Direct each child to horizontally fold a 9" white paper plate, then insert a gray pipe cleaner into one side and staple it to the side of the plate to represent the opossum's tail. 2. Cut the round center from a paper plate, fold it in half, and cut down the middle. Cut out a small half-moon shape from the straight side of one half. 3. Staple this shape to the large paper plate to represent the opossum's head. Then, cut out slits in the top of the opossum's body to represent fur. Next, cut one half-moon shape from the possum's body and two smaller half-moon shapes on both sides for the opossum's legs. Cut the remaining half of the small paper plate into two rectangular shapes, bend them in half and staple them to the back side of the opossum as a stand. 4. Have students cut out a pink nose, black eye, and black ear from construction paper and glue these in the appropriate places. Have students use silver or gray crayons to color the opossum's fur, whiskers, and toes.

Playin' Possum

Discuss how opossums have a special instinct which allows them to "play dead" if they are in danger. Animals who prey upon opossums and see the "dead" opossum usually ignore it and walk away. The opossum's instinct allows it to fall on its side with its mouth gaping open and its body limp and remain in this position until it thinks the danger is gone. Let the class play a game of "Possum" by having one player be the predator and the class be opossums. In an open area, have the "possums" scurry around (not too fast, as opossums move slowly!) in a designated area with the predator standing with his back to them. Tell the "predator" that he should shout "Play Possum," and count to five to give the opossums a five-second warning that "danger" is near! When the opossums hear the words, they should "play possum" by falling into a limp position. After the count of five, the predator should walk around the opossums to see if any move or make sounds. Those possums that move are "out"; those that remain "dead" continue in the game. Time the students for 1-2 minutes. After the time is up, the game begins again with the same child as the predator. When only one opossum remains "dead," that child becomes the new predator.

89

Wise Up About OWLS

Did You Know?

🌙 Owls have the best night vision of any creature on earth.

🌙 Owls have been called the "night watchman of our gardens" because they eat harmful rodents at night.

Whooo Are You?

Discuss with students how owls' eyes do not move, but owls can turn their heads 270° to see objects at the sides! Draw a large circle on the board and point to show just how far 270° is. Show students that a full circle rotation is 360° and a half circle rotation is 180°. Take the class outside to an area of blacktop or concrete where a chalk circle can be drawn. Have students help you draw a large circle on the concrete with chalk and mark 90°, 180°, 270°, and 360° in the appropriate places on the circle. Call on a student to stand in the center. Have the student play an owl by holding pieces of tagboard at the sides of her face so she cannot see to her sides. Explain that humans, unlike owls, can move their eyes from side to side and the tagboard will make their vision more like that of an owl. Quietly tell another student to stand at the 270° mark without revealing his identity to the "owl." Have the owl ask three yes/no questions to try to identify the mystery student. Then, allow the owl to make her guess and turn to the 270° mark to see if her guess is correct. Continue the game by allowing another student to be the owl.

Wise Owls

Owls are often used as a symbol for wisdom. Ancient Greeks believed the owl was sacred to Athena, their goddess of wisdom. Have students think about what wisdom an owl might share if it was able to speak. Then, give each student a copy of the owl pattern (page 92). Direct each student to write a sentence or two in a speech bubble cut from construction paper. Tell students that the sentences must be "spoken" from the owl's point of view and should be "wise" information about owls or other night animals. (If necessary, provide books and other materials for students to use as reference.)

After students have completed their sentences, have each color and cut out her owl pattern and speech bubble and glue the pieces to construction paper. Display the completed owls around the room or combine them into a class big book titled *Wise Owl Wisdom*.

Pine Cone Owls

Provide a pine cone for each student, along with craft feathers in natural colors for students to glue on the sides of their pine cones for the owls' wings. Cut feathers into small pieces that can be glued to the tops of the pine cones to represent the owls' ear tufts. Have each student glue two black felt circles on top of two larger yellow felt circles and then glue these on the pine cone for the owl's eyes. Next, provide a brown felt triangle shape for the student to glue on the pine cone for the owl's beak.

90

© Carson-Dellosa CD-2091

BANDITS of the NIGHT

Did You Know?

🌙 Raccoons are sometimes called "bandits" because of the black mask of fur around their eyes.

🌙 Raccoons have very sensitive paws, which they use to feel the shape and texture of objects.

🌙 Some people believe that a raccoon will wash its food in the water before eating, but what it is actually doing is getting the food wet to intensify the touch.

🌙 Raccoons have hand-like paws with long fingers that allow some to learn how to open cans, latches, and to get into all kinds of fun and trouble!

Raccoon Puppets

Let your little bandits make their own raccoon puppets! Provide each student with a lunch-size brown paper bag and a copy of the raccoon mask and tail patterns (page 92). Have the student color the face brown and the white parts of the tail brown. Then, have the student cut out and glue the mask to the flap of the bag and the tail to the opening on the back of the bag. Provide black construction paper for the students to cut triangles that they can glue to the front of the bags for arms. Let students use markers or crayons to add whiskers, noses, and mouths to their new furry friends.

Raccoon Treats

Your class will eat this snack like raccoons! Tell the class that raccoons are considered to be *omnivorous* which means they eat plants and animals. Blend together a "raccoon treat" for the students to sample. Mix together corn chips or corn cereal (to represent one of the raccoon's favorite treats–corn!), berries, nuts, sunflower seeds, and fish-shaped crackers (to represent another favorite–fish!). Before giving each student a small paper cup-full of the snack, discuss how raccoons use their strong sense of touch to identify food by its shape and texture before eating. Have students close their eyes and touch the food in their snack cups to see if they can identify the various foods.

Fact or Opinion?

Learn the truth about raccoons with this activity. After students have become familiar with information about raccoons, have some fun with fact and opinion statements. Write statements on copies of the raccoon mask pattern (page 92). Call on individual students to read a statement and then name whether the statement is a fact or an opinion. For example, opinion statements include, "Raccoons are cute." A fact is, "Baby raccoons are called cubs." Have the student tell how she determined which kind of statement she read.

COPY and CUT

raccoon mask

tail

owl
(use with bulletin board idea pg. 19)

Chung Yeung Festival

On the ninth day of the ninth lunar month, around the middle of October, many people in Hong Kong, which is in China, celebrate the Chung Yeung Festival. This celebration is based on the story of Woon King who lived during the Han Dynasty around 200 B.C. He was told in a dream to take his family to a high place to avoid a disaster. Woon King took his family to the hills and brought along a picnic to feed his family. Upon returning to the village, he found that it was in ruin from a flood. Today, the Chung Yeung Festival is considered a day of family remembrance and many families celebrate by picnicking in the mountains.

Family Memory Books

Let students honor their family memories with a family memory book. Provide each student with several sheets of white paper to fold in half. Staple the sheets of paper along the side, so they resemble pages of a book. Have students write and illustrate favorite family memories on each page. Give each student a piece of brown construction paper and have her make a cover for the book. Instruct students to draw picnic baskets on the covers of their books and title them *My Family Memories*. Let students take their books home to share with their families.

Go to the Top!

Eating cake called *ko* is customary during the Chung Yeung Festival. In Chinese, the word "ko" is a homophone for the word for "top." People in Hong Kong believe that anyone who eats the cake will be promoted to the top. Give a snack cake to each student. Have students write or tell what being on top means to them while the class enjoys the cakes!

Have a Picnic

Have a class picnic in honor of the Chung Yeung Festival. The day before the picnic, turn the classroom into a mountain range by having students draw pictures of mountains. Hang the pictures on the bulletin board and classroom walls so it feels as if the picnic is taking place on a mountain. Have each student bring in something for the picnic, such as bread, sandwich meat, soda, plates, potato chips, etc. Bring in blankets to spread on the floor and enjoy the view while eating a picnic lunch!

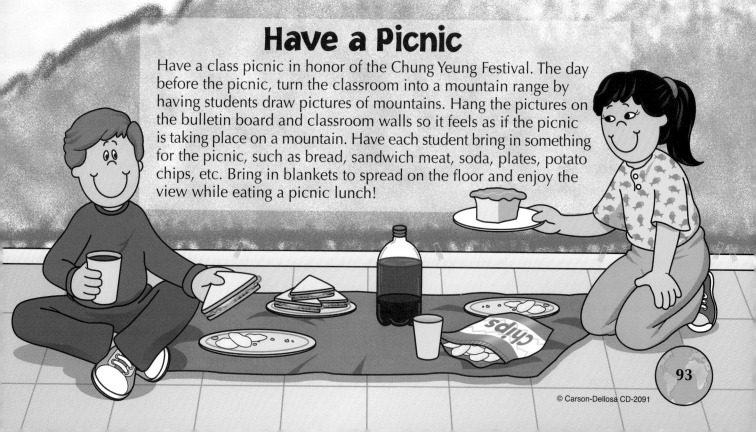

93

The Harvest Festival

In the Eastern European country of the Ukraine, much wheat is grown and communities all over the country join in celebration after the wheat crops have been harvested. Much wheat is grown in the Ukraine. The Harvest Festival usually takes place sometime in the middle of October. The festival has been celebrated for thousands of years as a way to express thanks for the bountiful harvest.

Neat Wheat Decorations

The Ukraine is known as the Bread Basket of Europe because of the large amount of wheat that is grown there. At the Harvest Festival people make decorations from wheat stalks. Provide each student with a large cardboard tube, construction paper, several lengths of thin yellow ribbon, glue, and scissors. If desired, use real wheat or raffia in place of the ribbon. Ask students to glue pieces of colored construction paper around their cardboard tubes. Then, have them tape the lengths of ribbon to the tops of the tubes. The teacher should run the ribbon over scissors so that it will curl. Next, have the students apply droplets of glue to the curly ribbons and sprinkle with glitter. Decorate the tubes with markers or crayons.

Wheat Sheaves

Have students draw outlines of wheat sheaves on pieces of white paper. At the top of the outline, have each student write *Wheat is used to make....* Provide newspapers and magazines and ask students to find foods that are made from wheat, such as bread, crackers, and cereals. Ask students to cut out the pictures and glue them inside the wheat outlines. As a finishing touch, provide each student with a piece of raffia to tie in a bow and glue around the middle of the wheat sheaf. Display the wheat sheaves on a bulletin board or wall.

Circle Dancing

At the Harvest Festival, children and adults participate in games and dances. Children play tug-of-war and hold sack races. One of the dances includes the circle dance. Play a lively tune and invite your students to participate in a circle dance. Ask students to form a circle and hold hands. Have them walk to the right. Once they've come full circle, have them walk full circle to the left. Then, at your signal, have the group stop, drop hands, spin around in place, and shout "Hooray!"

Trung Thu

Trung Thu (TROONG•thoo) is one mid-autumn festival in Vietnam that celebrates the beauty of the moon. It takes place on the 15th day of the eighth lunar month, which is usually in October. Festivities include family time when parents give their children treats and moon cakes, unicorn dancers (dancers with large masks who parade through the streets accompanied by drums and cymbals), wearing masks, and lighting lanterns.

A Taste of the Moon

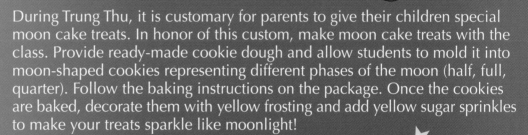

During Trung Thu, it is customary for parents to give their children special moon cake treats. In honor of this custom, make moon cake treats with the class. Provide ready-made cookie dough and allow students to mold it into moon-shaped cookies representing different phases of the moon (half, full, quarter). Follow the baking instructions on the package. Once the cookies are baked, decorate them with yellow frosting and add yellow sugar sprinkles to make your treats sparkle like moonlight!

Star Light, Star Bright

You'll be sure to see glowing faces when students make these Trung Thu star lanterns, which Vietnamese children carry during the festival parade. Provide students with stars cut from poster board or cardboard, different colors of plastic wrap, long cardboard tubes (candles), and art supplies, such as crayons, markers, glitter, etc. Have each student cover his star with colored plastic wrap (more than one color can be used). Then, allow the children to decorate their stars and cardboard tubes with the other materials. In Vietnam, children use real candles in their star lanterns, but have your students glue orange tissue paper to the tops of the tubes to resemble candles. Glue the cardboard tubes to the backs of the stars and have a star lantern procession!

Trung Thu (continued)

Unicorn Masks

During Trung Thu, unicorn dancers parade through the streets. Have students make their own unicorn masks. Give each student a large piece of construction paper. Provide glue, glitter, feathers, sequins, markers, crayons, etc., and have students decorate the paper. Then, have students cut out eye and mouth holes in their masks. Attach yarn to each side of the mask so children can wear them. Play some drum and cymbal music or let class musicians make their own music and let children don their masks and dance around, just like the unicorn dancers!

Set Sail!

Many children sail handmade boats on lakes during the Trung Thu festival. Have students make their own boats in honor of this tradition. Have each student bring in a shoebox. Provide yarn, cloth scraps, markers, lace, crayons, etc., and let students decorate their shoeboxes. Display the "boats" on a table covered with a blue tablecloth (water) during Trung Thu.

Moon Books

Let students celebrate the beauty of the moon and Trung Thu by making moon books. Provide students with several yellow construction paper circles to represent the moon. Provide crayons, markers, glue, etc., and have each student decorate one circle as a cover for his book. On the remaining circles, have students write reasons they think the moon is beautiful, such as "It lights up the dark sky, " or "It's big and orange sometimes." Have each student staple the circles together at the top. Display the moon books on a bulletin board during your study of Trung Thu.